Illuminated Lines

a pattern collection by
Kerin Dimeler-Laurence

Copyright 2014 © Knit Picks

All rights reserved. This book or any portion thereof may not be reproduced or used in any manner whatsoever without the express written permission of the publisher except for the use of brief quotations in a book review.

Printed in the United States of America

Second Printing, 2014

ISBN 978-1-62767-045-6

Versa Press, Inc
800-447-7829

www.versapress.com

CONTENTS

Morris Satchel — 6

Galloway Pullover — 18

Circlet Cardigan — 28

Glass Knot Afghan — 36

Monument Tam — 40

Fia Pullover — 44

MORRIS SATCHEL

by Kerin Dimeler-Laurence

FINISHED MEASUREMENTS
13x13x1"

YARN
Knit Picks Palette (100% Peruvian Highland Wool; 231 yards/50g):
MC Black 23729 3 balls, CC Celadon Heather 24254, CC Alfalfa 25097, CC Peapod 25098, CC Grass 24585, 1 ball each.

NEEDLES
US 1 (2.25 mm) 24" circular needles, or size to obtain gauge, and spare needle in same size
US 1 (2.25 mm) DPNs

NOTIONS
Yarn Needle
Stitch Markers
Smooth scrap yarn
Crochet hook for provisional CO
14" nylon zipper
48" of thin cotton cord to reinforce strap (optional)
Fabric and sewing thread for lining (optional)

GAUGE
32 sts and 32 rows = 4" in stranded St st in the round, blocked.

Morris Satchel

Notes:

Provisional Cast On (Crochet Chain method)
Using a crochet hook several sizes too big for the yarn, make a slipknot and chain for 1". Hold knitting needle in left hand. With yarn in back of the needle, work next chain st by pulling the yarn over the needle and through the chain st. Move yarn under and behind needle, and repeat for the number of sts required. Chain a few more sts off the needle, then break yarn and pull end through last chain. CO sts will be incorrectly mounted; knit into the back of these sts. To unravel (when sts need to be picked up), pull chain end out, and the chain should unravel, leaving live sts.

For video and photo tutorials for techniques such as Provisional Cast On, and Applied I-cord, visit the Knit Picks website at www.knitpicks.com/tutorials.

DIRECTIONS

This bag begins flat at the bottom and is then worked in the round to the upper edge.

Bottom

With scrap yarn and circular needles, Provisionally CO 107 sts. Attach MC and work in Garter st (knit every row) for 22 rows.

After the last of these rows, do not turn work. Instead, PM and PU and K one stitch in each Garter ridge along the adjacent short edge (11 sts). PM.

Unravel the Provisional CO and place 107 live sts on a spare needle. Knit directly from the live edge sts across these sts. PM, and PU and K 11 sts across the remaining short edge. There are now 236 sts on the needles. PM and begin working in the round.

Charts

Begin working from the charts around the bag: work from Border chart to first marker, Side chart to the second marker, Border chart to the third marker and Side chart to the end of round. Note that for each of these charts, the first round is completed in CC only.

Continue working from charts, switching contrast color around all charts as shown in the Border chart (all other charts are shown in two colors only).

Where noted on the Border chart, begin working from the Monogram or Alternate chart of your choice across the center 71 sts of the bag. Continue to switch CC colors as established, and work motif in MC.

Once you have worked through the Monogram portion, continue working just from the Border and Side charts through the last round.

BO stitches in MC.

Edging and Strap

The strap is worked as an Applied I-cord edge that is 'joined' into a larger cord at the Sides. With MC, and DPNs, begin working Applied I-cord around the bag, beginning on the center (6th) stitch of either Side:

To work Applied I-cord:
CO 4 sts.
*Knit three stitches and slip the fourth stitch knitwise.
PU and knit one more stitch from the edge. You will now have 5 stitches on your right needle.
Use your left needle tip to pass the slipped stitch over the last knitted stitch. This will leave you with four stitches on your right needle.
Slip these four stitches back onto the left needle tip purlwise, or slide to the other end of the needle. Tug on the working yarn to tighten up the stitches.
Repeat these steps from *.

Work around half of one Side, the front or back panel, and across the first five stitches of the second side. Break MC and place the four live stitches on scrap yarn.

Cast on 4 sts and begin a second Applied I-cord, working around the other half of the top edge. After the last round, do not break yarn.

At both sides, you should have four live stitches and the cast-on end of the other I-cord. Beginning after the last live stitch, PU 4 sts around the adjacent cast-on end. Join to work these 8 sts in the round. Work these 8 sts as I-cord or in the round on DPNs for 48" (this will make a strap long enough to wear cross-body) or desired strap length. If you wish to reinforce the strap with cord, you can pin the cord inside the end of the strap and knit around the cord, or you can knit the strap and insert the cord afterwards.

After the last round, break yarn, leaving a 12" tail.

If you have not already done so, insert the cord into the strap. This can be done by taping the cord to one end of a long circular needle, and using it as a guide; or, use an elastic or drawstring threading tool.

Using the yarn tail, graft the 8 live sts to the four live sts and CO end of the other side of the edge.

Finishing

Using a yarn needle and MC, stitch through the strap and cord to secure the cord. Weave in ends, wash and block.

Zipper
Sew the zipper in place across the top border.

Lining
Using the bag as a guide, cut and sew a lining for the bag; whipstitch in place over the zipper tape.

Border

Work from the Alphabet or Alternate Pattern chart of your choice over these 71 sts and 71 rounds (area bounded in red).

Work the border pattern on both sides of the bag.

Side

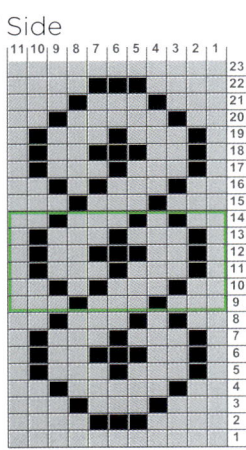

Repeat rounds 9-14 15 times.

Alternate Pattern 1 - Maze

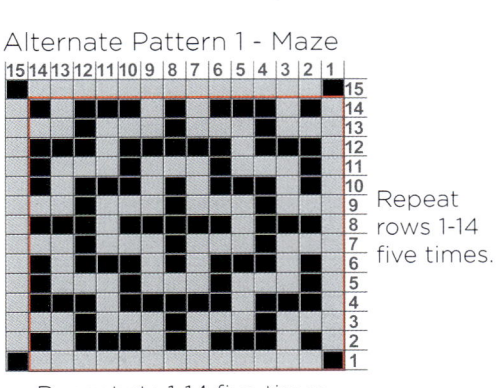

Repeat rows 1-14 five times.

Repeat sts 1-14 five times.

Alternate Pattern 1 - Keys

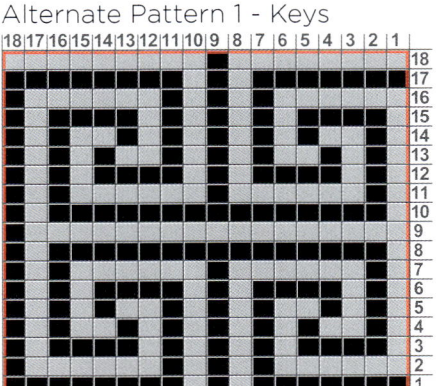

Repeat rounds 1-18 3 times, then work sts 1-17.

Repeat sts 1-18 3 times, then work sts 1-17.

Morris Satchel | 9

Alternate Pattern 3 - Weave

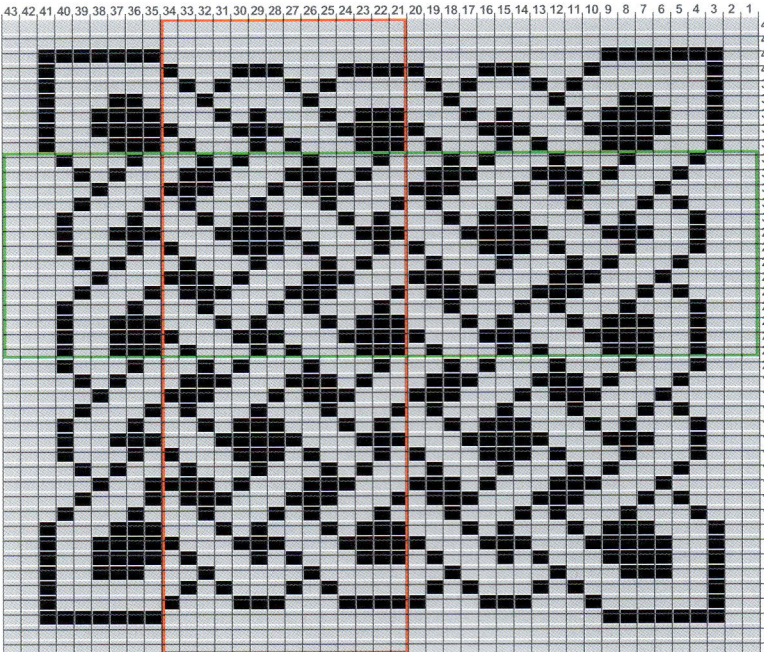

Repeat rows 21-34 four times.

Repeat sts 21-34 (red outline) four times.

Alternate Pattern 4 - Spirals

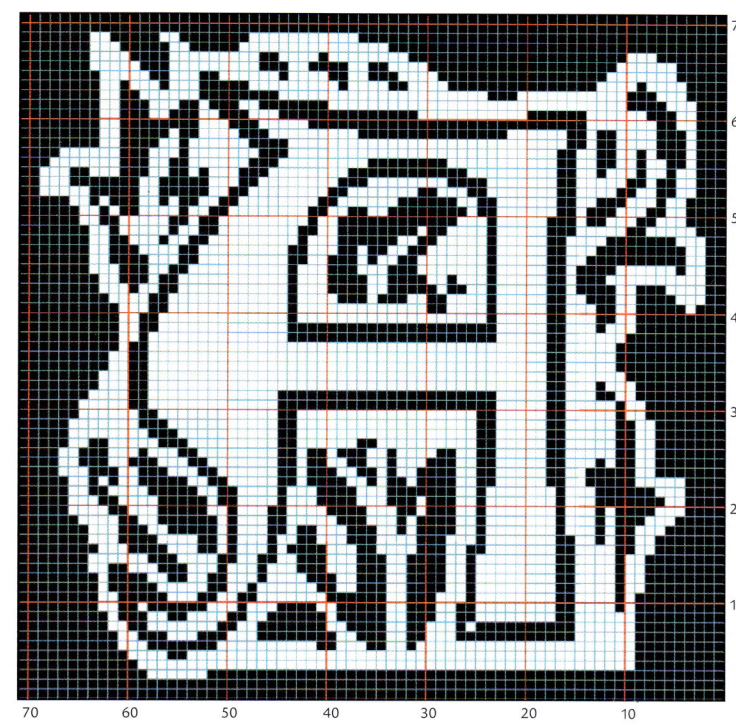

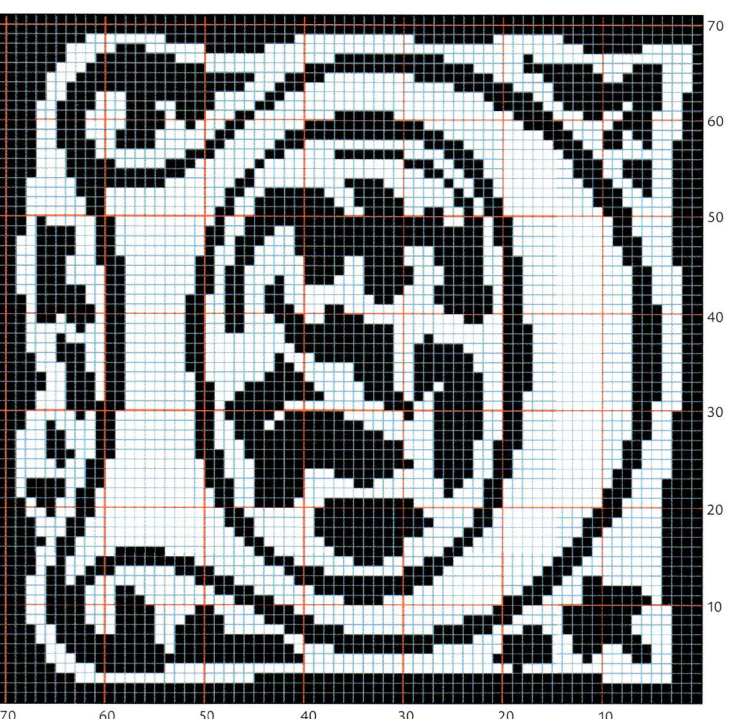

Morris Satchel | 11

Morris Satchel

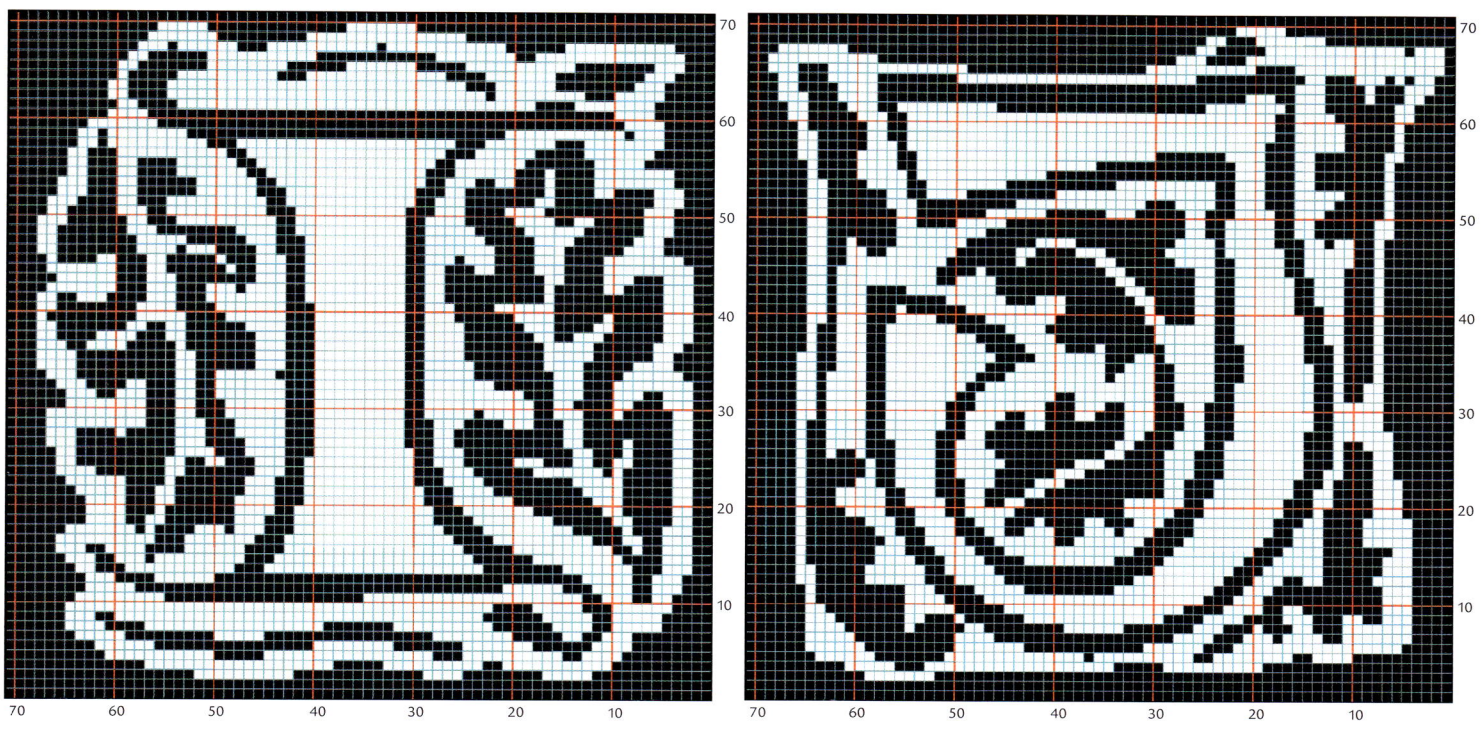
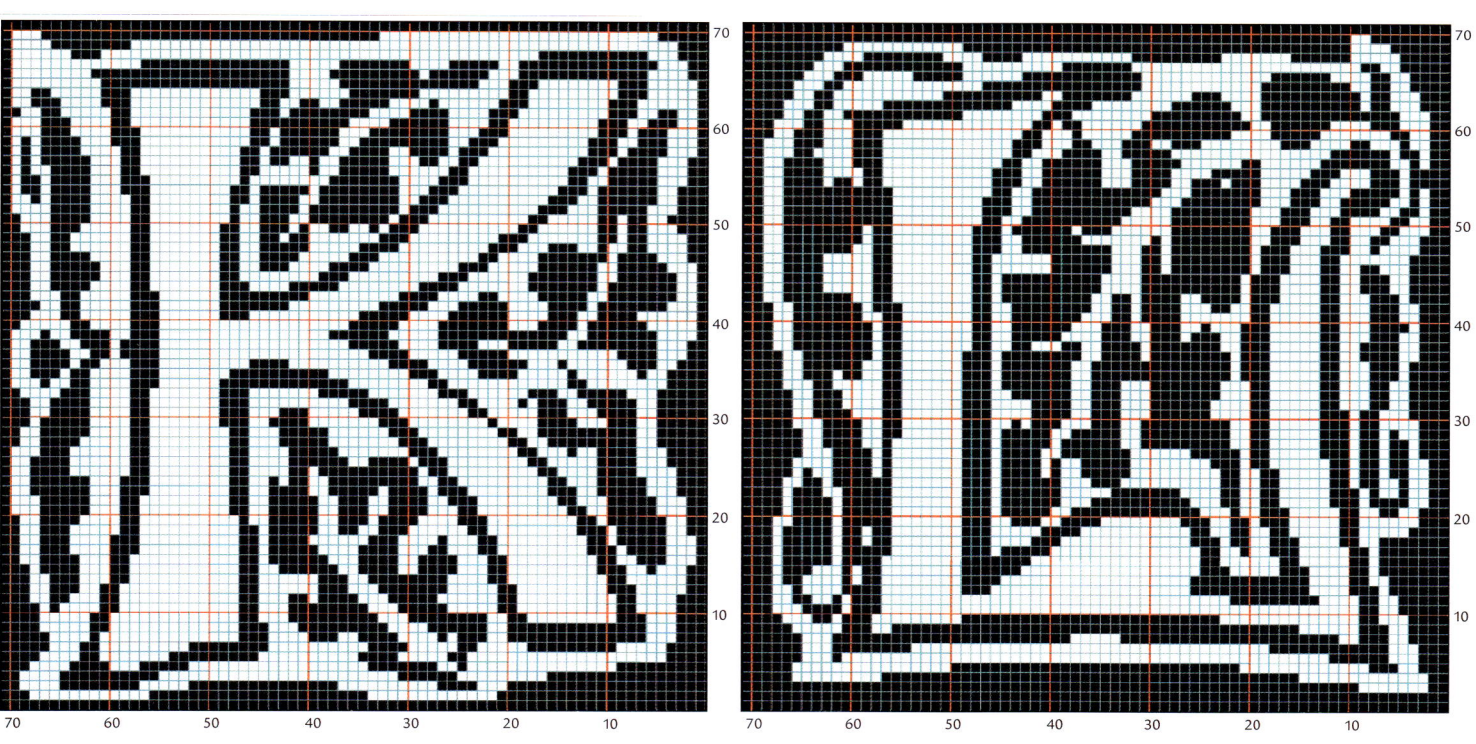

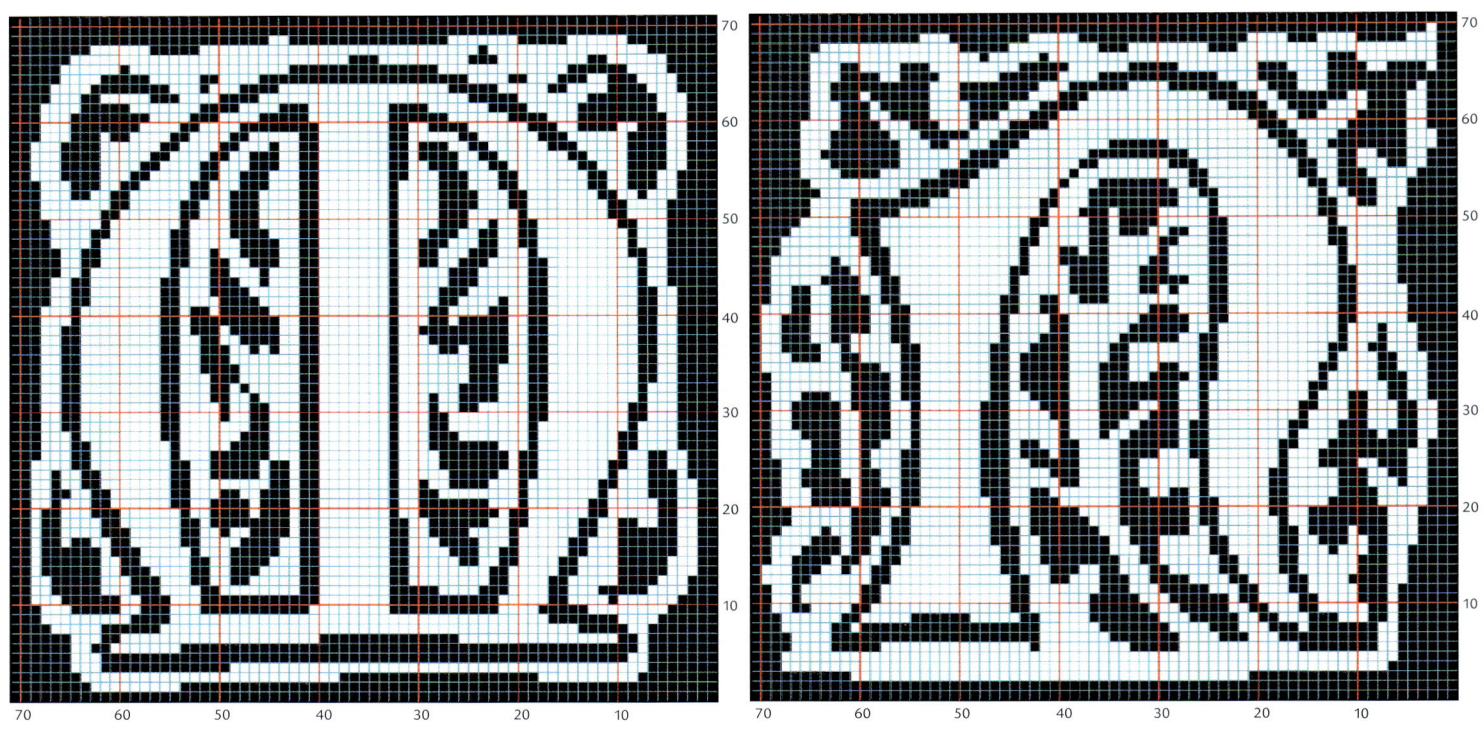
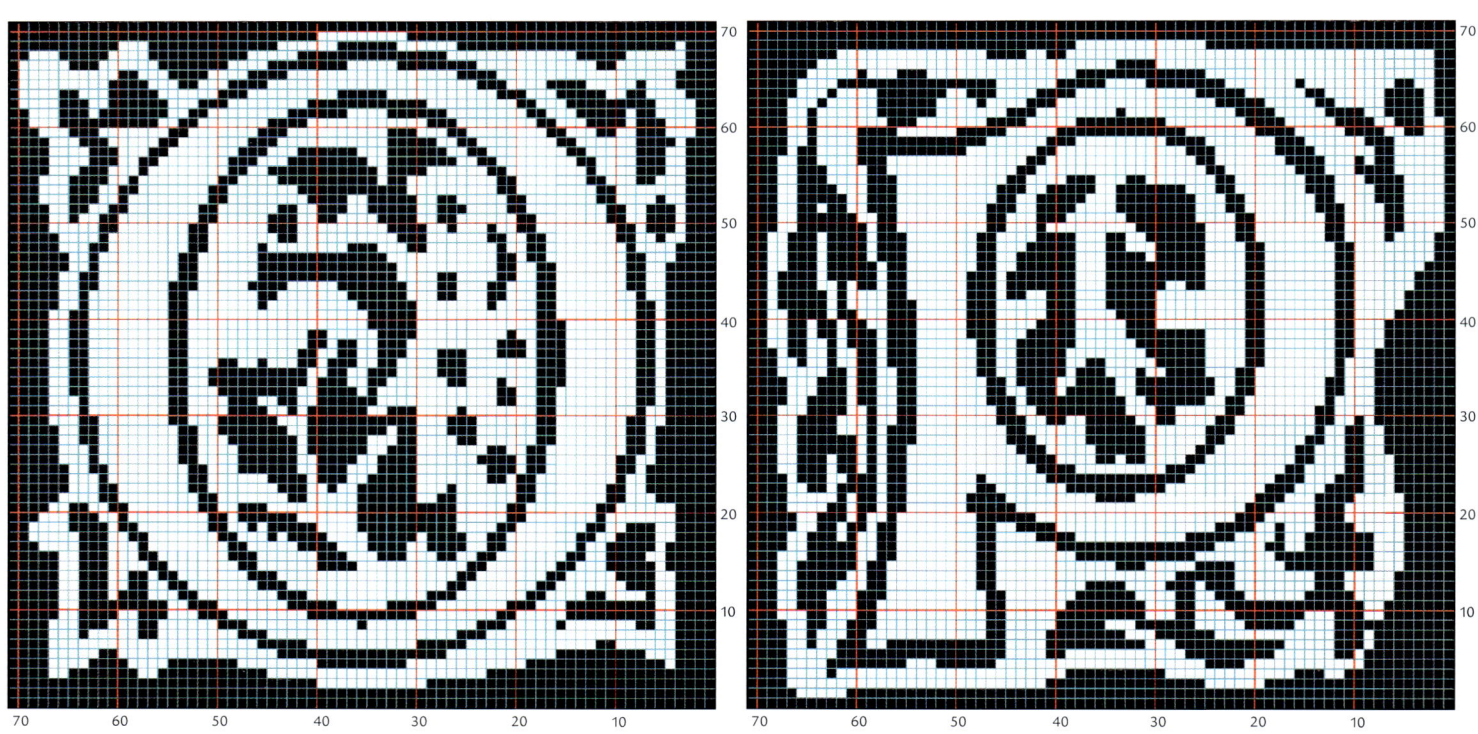

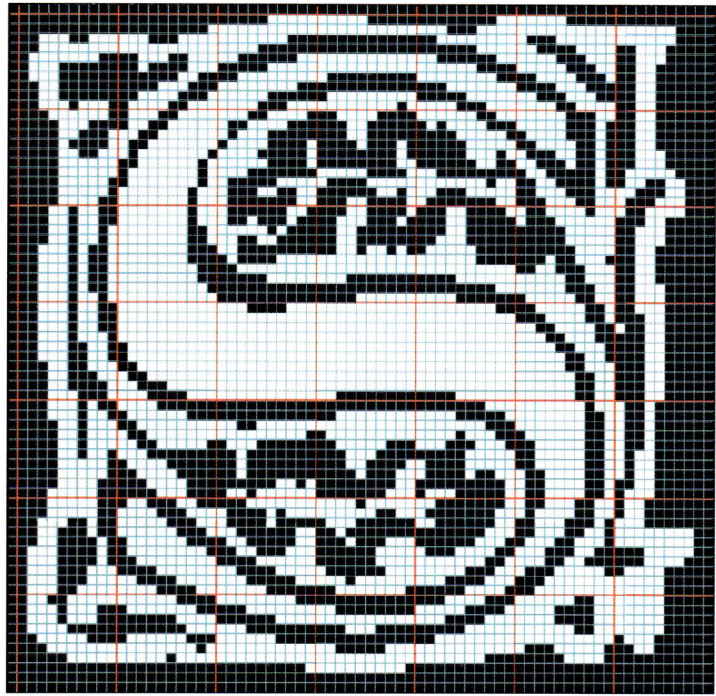

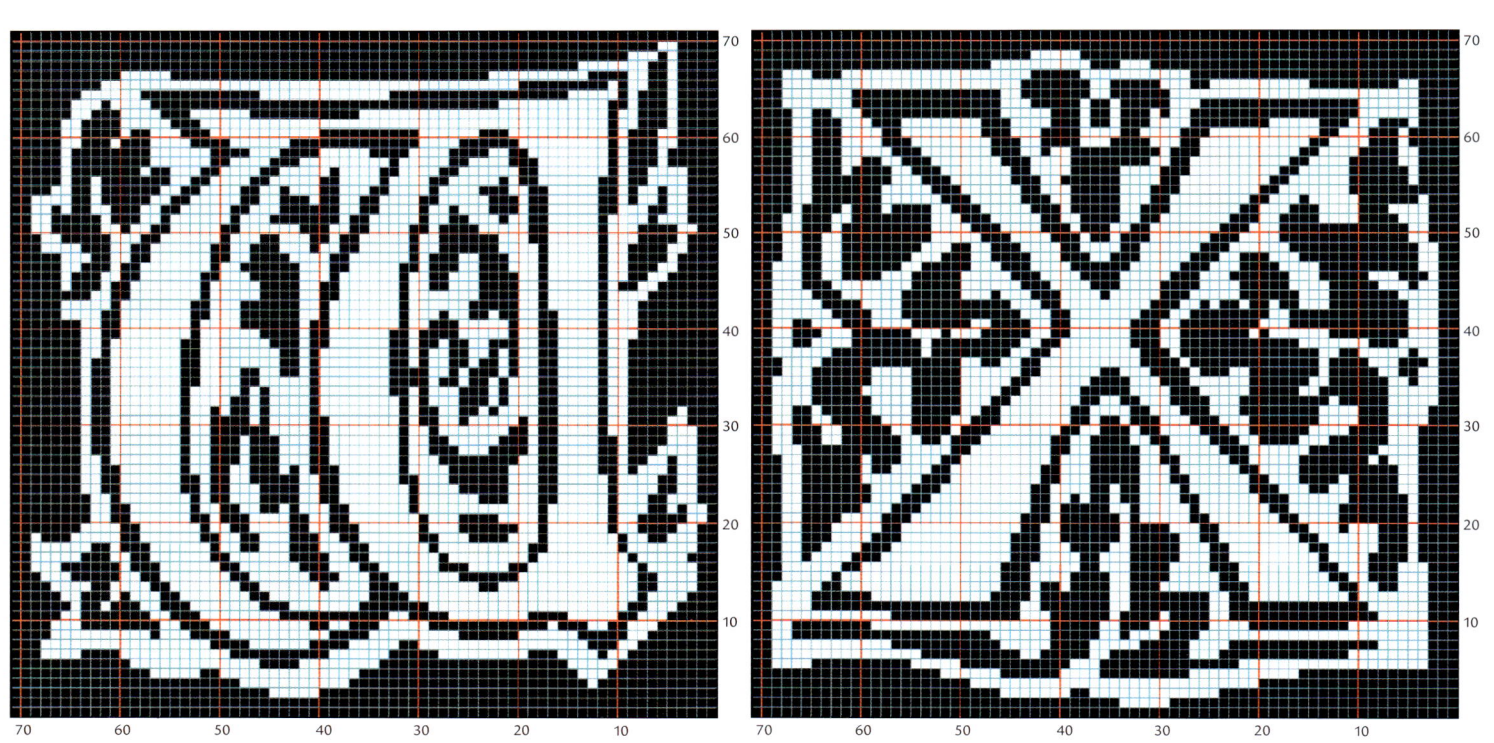

16 | Morris Satchel

70
60
50
40
30
20
10
60
50
40
30
20
10

70
60
50
40
30
20
10
70
60
50
40
30
20
10

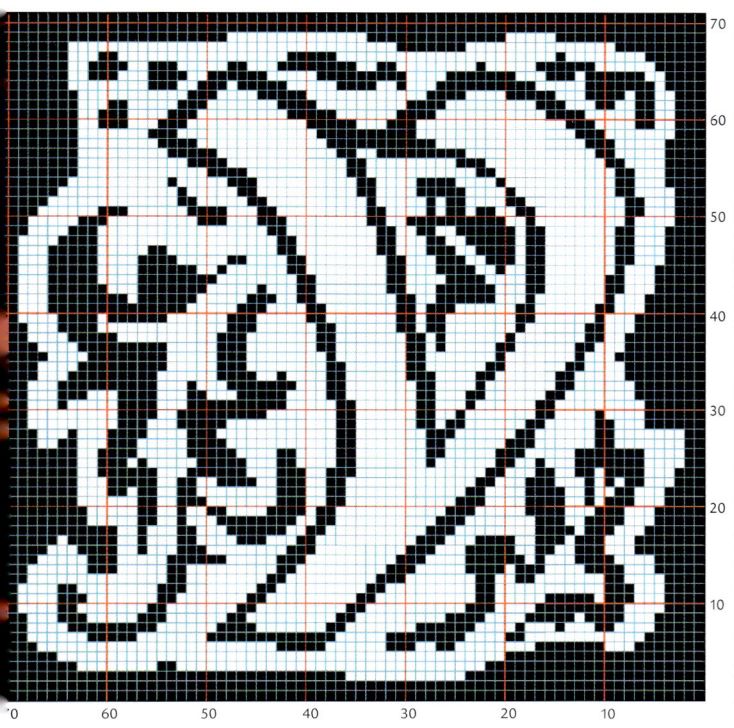

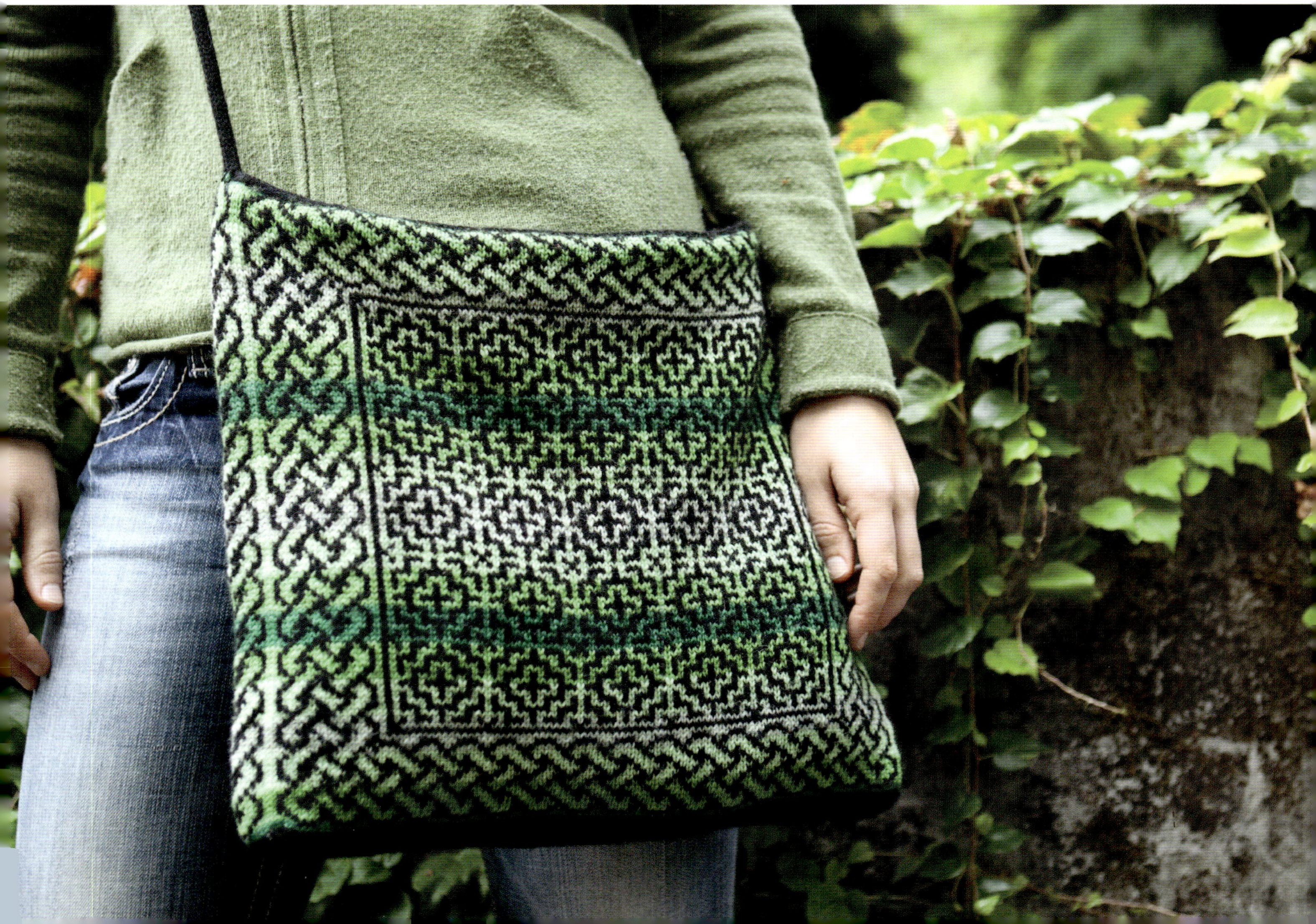

GALLOWAY PULLOVER
by Kerin Dimeler-Laurence

Finished Measurements
32 (36, 40, 44, 48, 52, 56, 60, 64)" Finished chest circumference

Yarn
Knit Picks Wool of the Andes Tweed (80% Peruvian Highland Wool, 20% Donegal Tweed; 110 yards/50g): Down Heather 25458, 10 (12, 14, 16, 18, 22, 24, 26, 28) balls.

Needles
US 7 (4.5mm) 24-32" circular needles and DPNs, or 40" or longer circulars for Magic Loop, or size to obtain gauge

Circular needles and DPNs or long circular needles for Magic Loop two sizes smaller than those used to obtain gauge

Notions
Yarn Needle
Stitch Markers
Cable Needle
Stitch Holder or Scrap Yarn

Gauge
18 sts and 32 rows = 4" in seed stitch on larger needles, blocked.
26 sts and 32 rows = 4" in cable pattern on larger needles, blocked.

Galloway Pullover

Notes:

Wrap and Turn
Work until the stitch to be wrapped. If knitting: bring yarn to the front of the work, slip next st as if to purl, return the yarn to the back; turn work and slip wrapped st onto RH needle. Continue across row. If purling: bring yarn to the back of the work, slip next st as if to purl, return the yarn to the front; turn work and slip wrapped st onto RH needle. Continue across row.

Picking up wraps:
Work to the wrapped st. If knitting, insert the RH needle under the wrap(s), then through the wrapped st K-wise. Knit the wrap(s) together with the wrapped st. If Purling, slip the wrapped st P-wise onto the RH needle, and use the LH needle to lift the wrap(s) and place them on the RH needle. Slip wrap(s) and unworked st back to LH needle; purl all together through the back loop.

Centered Double Increase (CDI)
Knit into the back of the stitch, then into the front of the same stitch. Knit into the vertical bar between these two sts, which are now on the RH needle. The bar is the stitch you knit into the back and front of originally.

Seed Stitch
Round 1: *K1, P1. Repeat from * to end of round.
Round 2: * P1, K1. Repeat from * to end of round.

M1L (Make 1 Left-leaning stitch)
PU the bar between st just worked and next st and place on LH needle as a regular stitch; knit through the back loop.

M1R (Make 1 Right-leaning stitch)
PU the bar between st just worked and next st and place on LH needle backwards (incorrect stitch mount). Knit through the front loop.

3-Needle Bind Off
Hold the two pieces of knitting together with the needle points facing to the right. Insert a third needle into the first stitch on each of the needles knitwise, starting with the front needle. Work a knit stitch, pulling the loop through both of the stitches you've inserted the third needle through. After you've pulled the loop through, slip the first stitch off of each of the needles. This takes two stitches (one from the front needle and one from the back) and joins them to make one finished stitch on the third needle (held in your right hand). Repeat this motion, inserting your needle into one stitch on the front and back needles, knitting them together and slipping them off of the needles. Each time you complete a second stitch, pass the first finished stitch over the second and off of the needle (as you would in a traditional bind-off).

For video and photo tutorials for these and other techniques such as the Mattress stitch, visit the Knit Picks website at http://www.knitpicks.com/tutorials.

Before beginning, read through the directions carefully, underlining or highlighting information for your size, and check for work happening "at the same time."

DIRECTIONS
Sleeves
The sleeves are knit identically and can be worked separately or both at the same time using the Magic Loop method. They are worked in the round to the sleeve cap, then worked flat to the top. The cable patterning on the sleeves is a simplified version of the main body cable on the sweater. Stitches are added after the cuff to allow the cable pattern to lie flat. The sleeve increases take place in the Seed stitch that runs across the underside.

With smaller needles, CO 34 (36, 38, 40, 42, 46, 50, 52, 54) sts. PM and join to work in the round, being careful not to twist sts. Work in K1, P1 rib around all sts for 16 rounds, placing second marker after 17 (18, 19, 20, 21, 23, 25, 26, 27) sts to mark the center of the sleeve.

Switch to larger needles and work a set-up round:
Work 1 (2, 3, 4, 5, 7, 9, 10, 11) sts in Seed st. PM to mark beginning of cable panel. Increase for cable panel: KFB twice, P 2 (2, 3, 3, 4, 4, 4, 4), work a Centered Double Increase 1 (1, 1, 1, 1, 2, 2, 2, 2) times, P 6 (6, 3, 3, 3, 4, 1, 1, 4), work a CDI 2 (2, 1, 1, 1, 1, 1, 1, 1) times, work 6 sts in Seed st (6 sts in Seed st, P5, P5, P5, 6 sts in Seed st, 12 sts in Seed st, 12 sts in Seed st, 6 sts in Seed st), work a CDI 2 (2, 2, 2, 2, 1, 1, 1, 1) times, P (6, 6, 5, 5, 5, 4, 1, 1, 4), work a CDI 1 (1, 1, 1, 1, 2, 2, 2, 2) times, [sizes 40, 44, 48 only: P3, work a CDI once], P 2 (2, 3, 3, 3, 4, 4, 4, 4), KFB twice. PM and work in Seed st to end of round. 14 sts increased across the cable panel; 50 (52, 54, 56, 58, 62, 66, 68, 70) sts total.

Begin working from Sleeve chart at the round indicated for your size, following repeats as shown and working the outer edges in Seed stitch. *At the same time*, work increases as given below. After the last round for your size, move on to the Sleeve Cap chart.

Sleeve Increases
Increase Round: KFB in the first and last sts of the round: 2 sts added.

Size 56: Work an Increase Round on the first round.

All sizes: Work an Increase Round every 11th (8th, 7th and 15th, 7th, 6th, 4th and 9th, 4th and 9th, 4th, 4th) round 11 (14, 8, 18, 21, 14, 14, 31, 32) times. Work 3 (12, 8, 2, 2, 6, 10, 12, 4) rounds in pattern. You should be at the end of the last repeat of the Sleeve Chart. 72 (80, 86, 92, 100, 118, 124, 130, 134) sts on the needles.

Sleeve Cap
The sleeve caps are shaped with bound off stitches and decreases. Round 1 is the last round – the rest of the cap is worked flat.

On round 1, work in pattern to 3 (3, 4, 5, 6, 10, 10, 11, 10) sts before the end of the round. Bind off the last 3 (3, 4, 5, 6, 10, 10, 11, 10) sts and the first 3 (3, 4, 5, 6, 10, 10, 11, 10) sts of RS row 2 (shown on chart). Begin working from row 2 of the Sleeve Cap chart, repeating decreases shown on the right side of the cap on the left side as well.

After the last row for your size, BO all remaining sts.

Sleeve

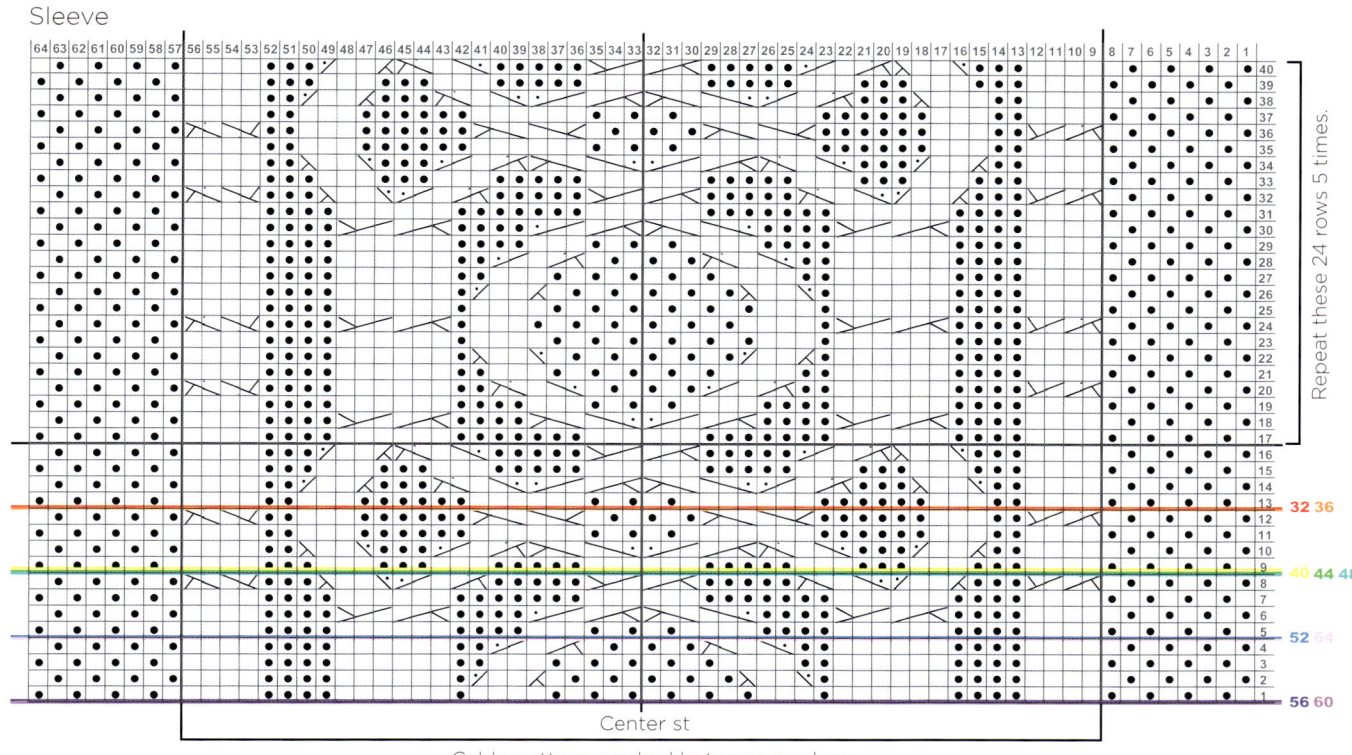

Cable pattern, worked between markers

All rounds are read right to left.

Seed stitch panels on this chart are for reference; sleeve increases are worked in seed stitch and the cable pattern centered on the sleeve.

Legend

When knitting in the round all stitches are worked as RS.

- **knit** — RS knit, WS purl
- **purl** — WS purl, WS knit
- **no stitch** — Placeholder - No stitch made.
- **make one right** — See instructions in pattern
- **(k1 p1 k1) in 1 st** — knit, purl and knit again all in the same st to make 3 sts from 1
- **make one left** — See instructions in pattern
- **(k1 yo k1) in 1 st** — k1 leave on needle, yo, then knit again into same st to make 3 sts from 1; (P1, yo, p1) into 1 st on WS
- **knit tbl** — Knit stitch through back loop
- **k7tog** — Knit seven sts together as one; WS, purl 7 sts tog as one.
- **Wrap & Turn (W&T)** — See instructions in pattern.
- **bind off**

- **c2 over 2 right** — sl2 to CN, hold in back. k2, k2 from CN
- **c3 over 3 left** — sl3 to CN, hold in front. k3, k3 from CN
- **c3 over 3 right** — sl3 to CN, hold in back. k3, then k3 from CN
- **c3 over 3 right P** — sl3 to CN, hold in back. k3 then p3 from
- **c3 over 3 left P** — sl3 to CN, hold in front. p3, k3 from CN
- **c2 over 2 left** — sl 2 to CN, hold in front. k2, k2 from CN
- **c3 over 2 right P** — sl2 to CN, hold in back. k3, then p2 from
- **c3 over 2 left P** — sl3 to CN, hold in front. p2, then k3 from
- **c3 over 1 right P** — sl1 to CN, hold in back. k3, p1 from CN
- **c3 over 1 left P** — sl3 to CN, hold in front. p1, k3 from CN

Galloway Pullover | 21

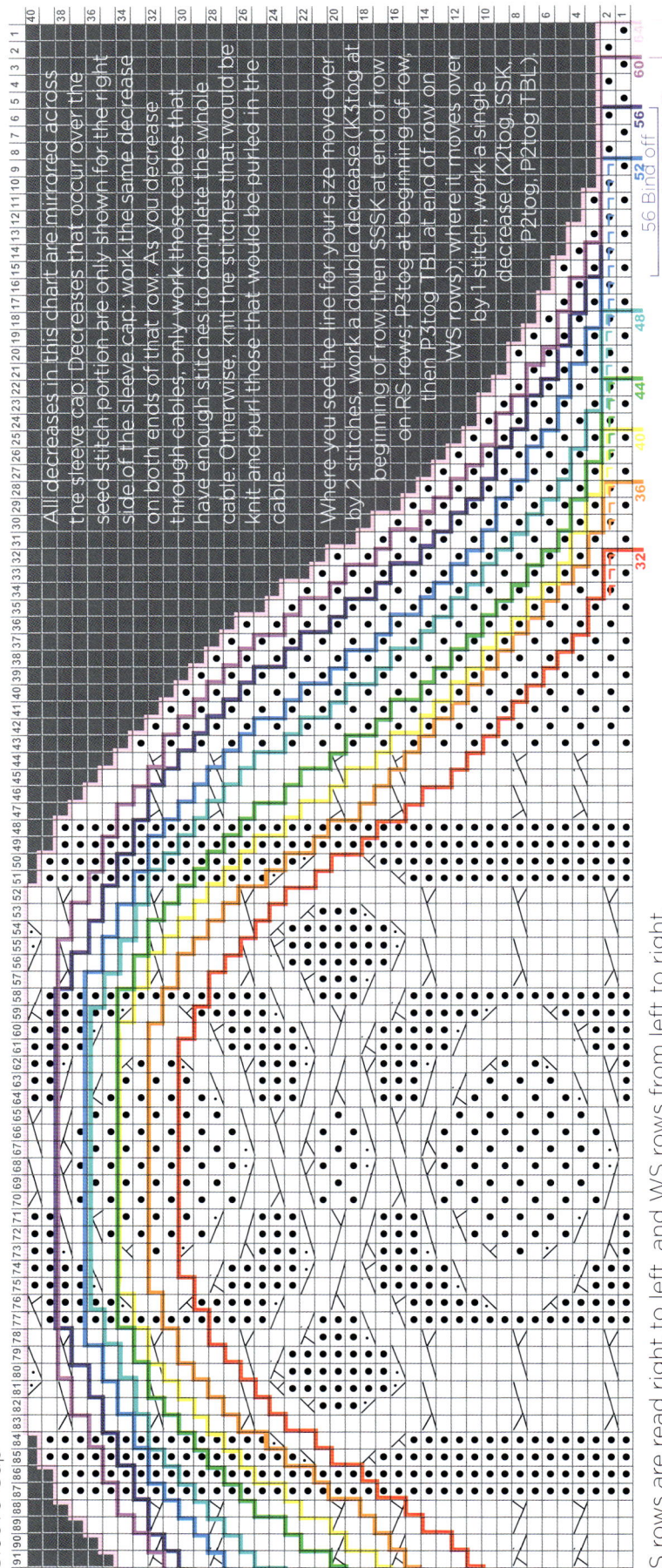

Body

The body is worked in the round to the armscyes; the front and back are then worked separately to the shoulders.

With smaller needles, CO 144 (162, 180, 198, 216, 234, 252, 270, 288) sts. PM and join to work in the round, being careful not to twist sts. Work in K1, P1 rib around all sts for 16 rounds. Knit one round, placing marker after 72 (81, 90, 99, 108, 117, 126, 135, 144) sts; this will mark the Right underarm.

Switch to larger needles and work a set-up round. This will increase the front and back of the body over the cabled sections.

Body Set-up Round: *Work 5 (6, 9, 12, 14, 14, 17, 19, 24) sts in Seed st. PM to mark beginning of cable panel. Over the next 62 (69, 72, 75, 80, 89, 92, 97, 96) sts, increase, according to size, as follows:

32: KFB 3 times, (K1, KFB) 28 times, KFB 3 times. 34 sts increased.

36: K2, [(KFB, K1) twice, KFB] 13 times, K2. 39 sts increased.

40: (KFB twice, K1) 24 times. 48 sts increased.

44: KFB 3 times, (K1, KFB 3 times) 18 times. 57 sts increased.

48: K1, (KFB twice, K1) 26 times, K1. 52 sts increased.

52: [(KFB, K1) 3 times, KFB twice] 11 times, K1. 55 sts increased.

56: [(KFB, K1) 5 times, KFB 3 times, (K1, KFB) 5 times] 4 times. 52 sts increased.

60: KFB, [(KFB, K1) twice, KFB] 19 times, KFB. 59 sts increased.

64: [(KFB, K1) twice, KFB] 19 times, KFB 3 times. 60 sts increased.

There are now 96 (108, 120, 132, 132, 144, 144, 156, 156) sts across the cable panel. PM and work in Seed st over the remaining 5 (6, 9, 12, 14, 14, 17, 19, 24) sts to the Right underarm marker.

Repeat from * across Back. 106 (120, 138, 156, 160, 172, 178, 194, 204) sts across both Front and Back. 212 (240, 276, 312, 320, 344, 356, 388, 408) sts total.

On the next round, begin working from the Body chart between cable panel markers, starting at the round indicated for your size and working repeats as shown. After all chart repeats have been worked, move on to the Upper Front and Back chart and begin shaping the armscyes and neckline.

Armscye Shaping

On the next round, work across Seed st panel and then across first round of the Upper Front and Back chart. Work in Seed st to 2 (2, 3, 4, 4, 4, 5, 5, 6) sts before Right underarm marker. BO the next

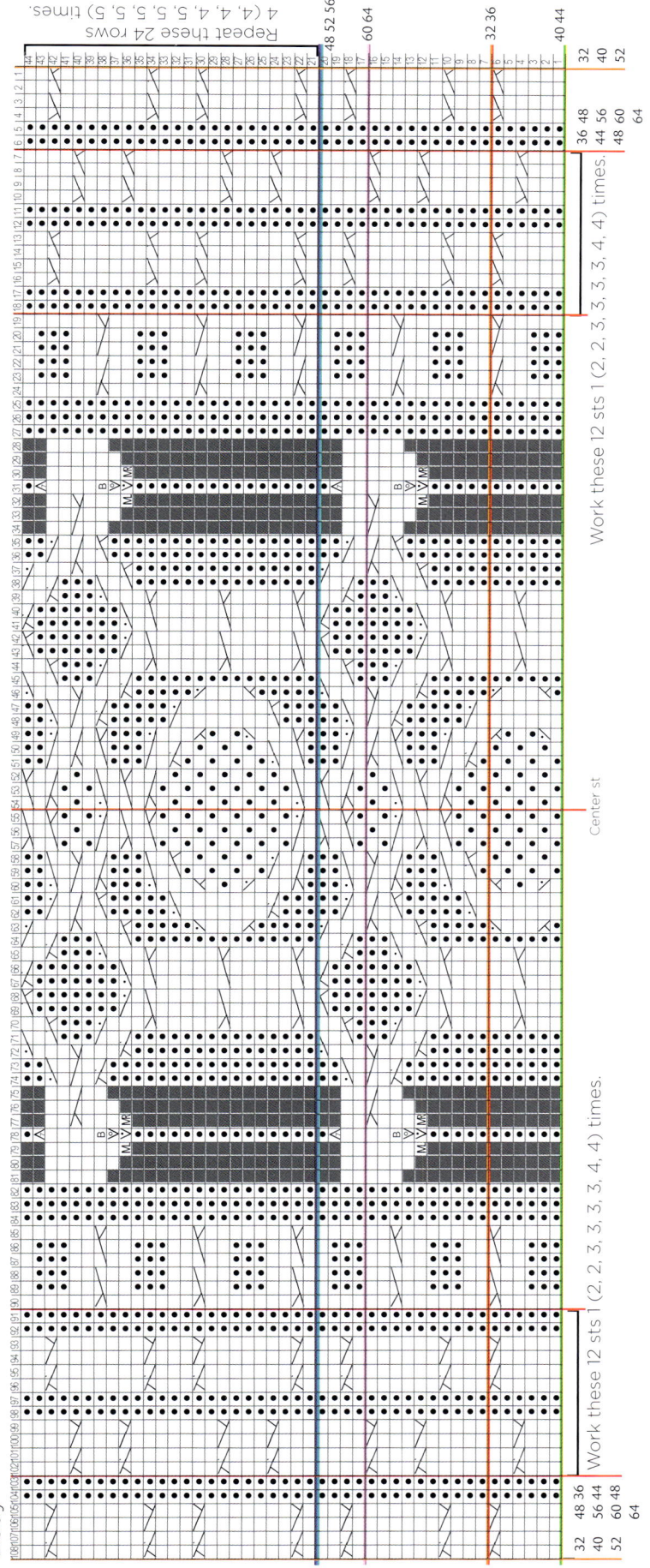

4 (4, 6, 8, 8, 8, 10, 10, 12) sts, removing marker. Work across Back from first round of the Upper Front and Back chart. Work in Seed st to 2 (2, 3, 4, 4, 4, 5, 5, 6) sts before the end of the round; BO the last 2 (2, 3, 4, 4, 4, 5, 5, 6) sts, remove marker, and BO the first 2 (2, 3, 4, 4, 4, 5, 5, 6) sts of the next round. Place all Back sts on a holder or scrap yarn. Armscye decreases and neckline decreases happen at the same time; BO sts at neckline where indicated in the chart, attach a second ball of yarn, and work left and right sides of the Front. All neckline decreases are represented in the chart.

Armscye Decreases

While maintaining pattern as shown in Upper Front and Back chart, K2tog at each armscye edge on the next row, and then:

32: Every other row twice.

36: On the next row, then every other row twice.

40: On the next row, then every other row twice, then every third row twice.

44: On the next two rows, then every other row three times, then every third row twice.

48: On the next three rows, then every other row three times, then every third row three times.

52: On the next three rows, then every other row three times, then every third row three times.

56: On the next four rows, then every other row three times, then every third row three times, then on the fifth row.

60: On the next four rows, then every other row four times, then every third row three times, then every fifth row twice.

64: On the next five rows, then every other row four times, then every third row four times, then on the fourth row twice, then on the fifth row twice.

All of the Seed sts of the gusset should now be removed.

Continue working Front to the shoulders following the Upper Front and Back chart.

Back

Place held Back sts on needles. Attach yarn with RS facing, and, maintaining pattern as shown in Upper Front and Back chart, K2tog at each armscye edge on the next row and then work row 2 of chart.

Continue working flat, working Armscye Decreases as done for the Front, and working from Upper Front and Back chart to the shoulders. On the last row for your size, BO all back neck sts (denoted by thin border line on chart), leaving the shoulder sts live.

Assembly

After completing all charts, assemble the sweater pieces.

Turn the sweater inside out. Place matching Front and Back shoulders on needles, holding one side in front of

Galloway Pullover | 23

Upper Front and Back (continued)

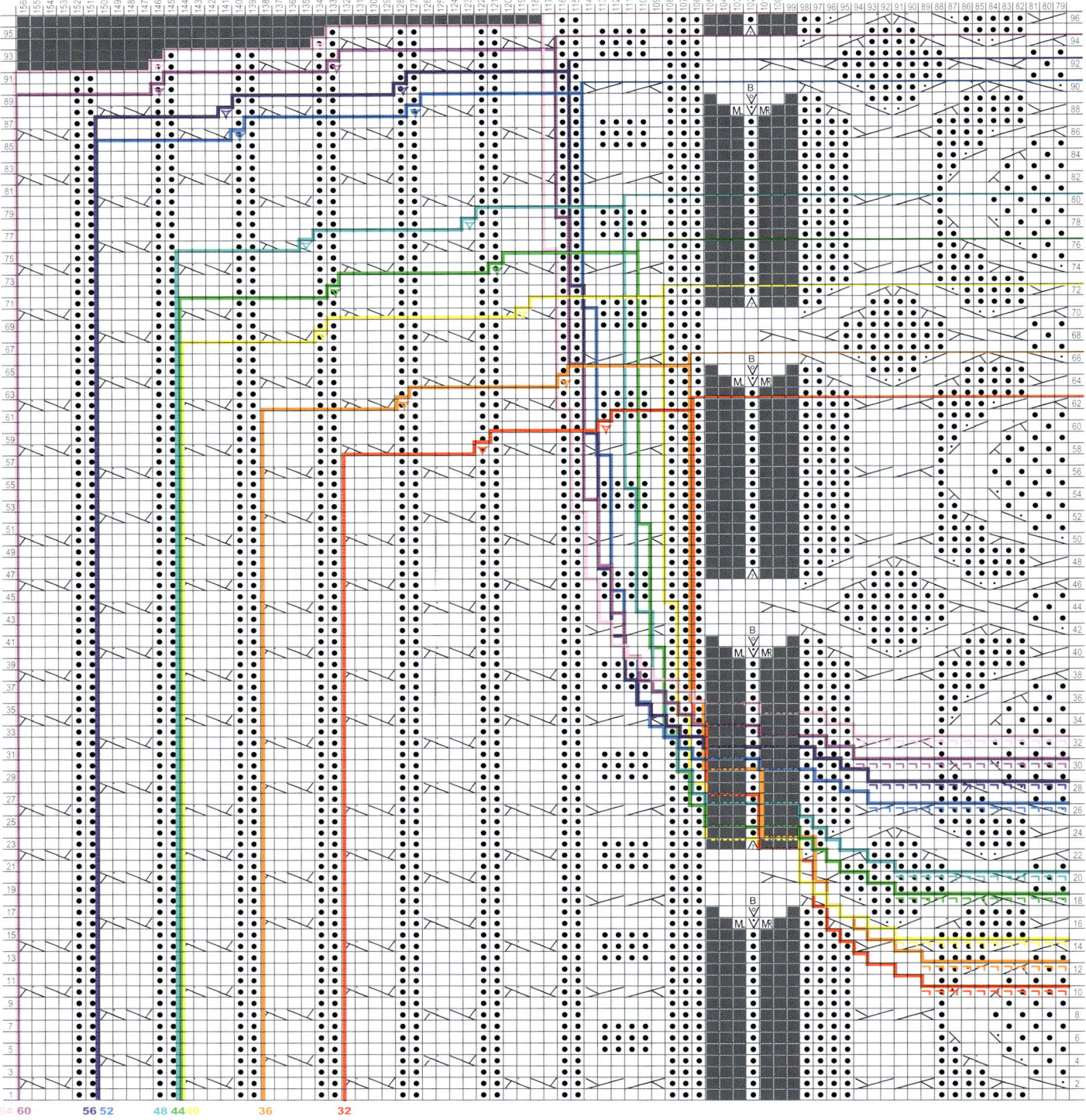

When knitting flat RS rows are read right to left, and WS rows from left to right.

All decreases in this chart are mirrored across the neckline. As you decrease through cables, only work those cables that have enough stitches to complete the whole cable. Otherwise, knit the sts that would be knit and purl those that would be purled in the cable.

Where you see the line for your size move over by 2 stitches, work a double decrease (K3tog, SSSK, P3tog, P3tog TBL); where it moves over by 1 stitch, work a single decrease (K2tog, SSK, P2tog, P2tog TBL).

Galloway Pullover

Upper Front and Back

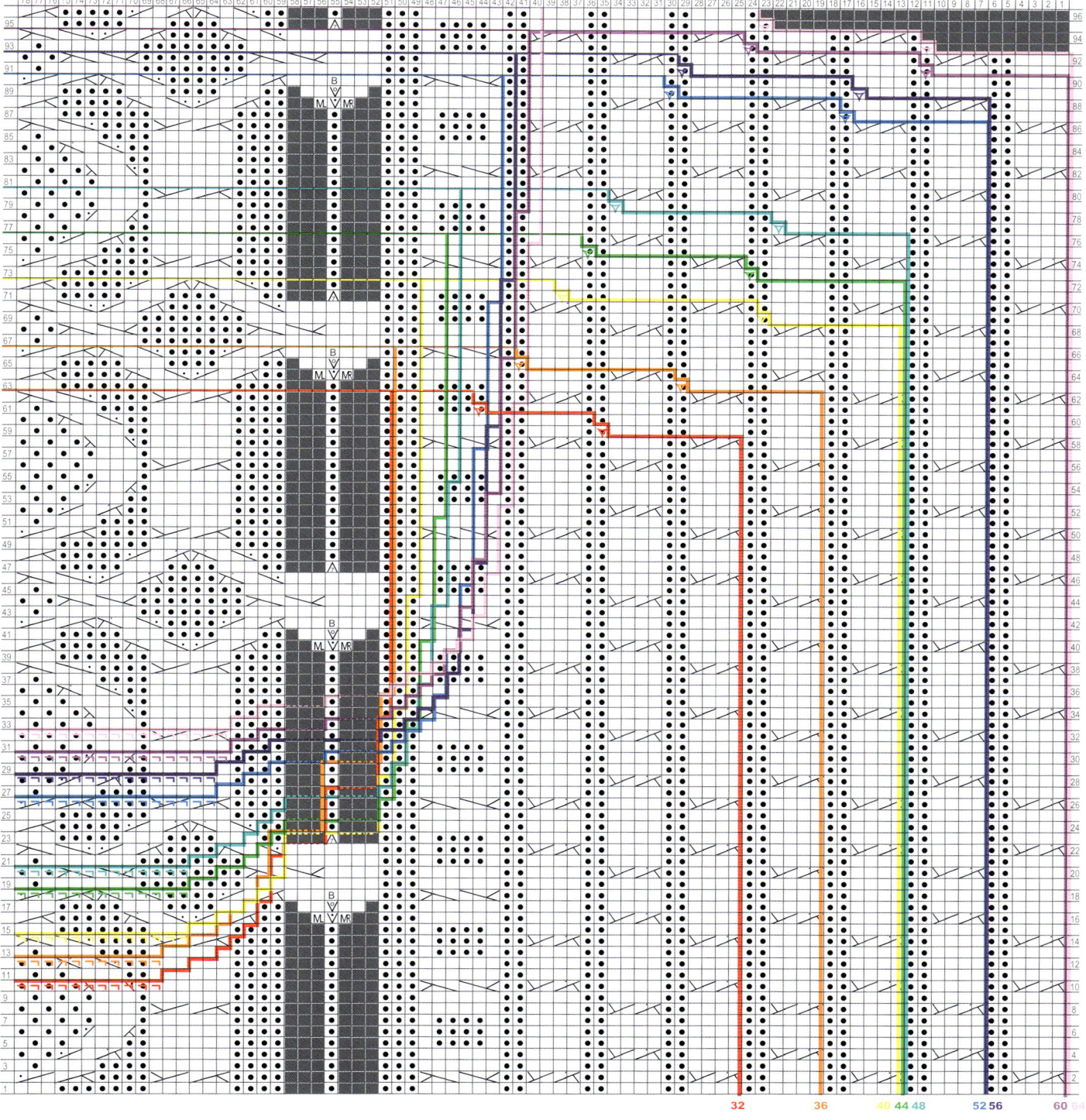

Galloway Pullover | 25

the other, right sides together. Perform a 3-needle BO across all sts using the yarn tail from either side. Repeat for other shoulder.

Set in Sleeves
With right sides facing out, set sleeves into armscye openings, making sure that the center of each sleeve cap is placed at the shoulder seam and that the bound off stitches for both sleeve and armscye are centered. Pin in place. Using yarn needle and yarn, begin at the underarm and sew sleeves into the armscyes, using Mattress stitch.

Collar Options
This sweater has two options for finishing the neckline: A rolled ribbed hem, or a shawl collar.

Shawl Collar
The shawl collar is picked up around the neckline and attached in an overlap at the center front.

With smaller needles and RS facing, PU sts around the neckline: Starting at the first st to the right of the open cable on the Right Front shoulder (st 105 on the Upper Front and Back chart), PU and work in Seed st 16 (17, 25, 28, 29, 33, 33, 33, 33) sts to shoulder, PM and PU 30 (30, 33, 36, 37, 42, 43, 44, 44) sts across bound off sts at back neck, PM and PU 16 (17, 25, 28, 29, 33, 33, 33, 33) sts down front Left neckline to the last st before the closed cables (st 50 on the Upper Front and Back chart). 62 (64, 83, 92, 95, 108, 109, 110, 110) total sts.

Collar Increase row: KFB, work in Seed st as established to last st, KFB.

Work in Seed st, working a Collar Increase row every row 10 times, then every other row until there are 29 (30, 32, 32, 34, 34, 36, 36, 36) sts between the markers and the ends of the row. Continue working flat in Seed st until collar overlaps completely across bound off sts at front neckline. BO all sts loosely.

Attach collar to front neckline: lay Left side of collar across bound off sts at neckline so that the collar bind off lines up with the last bound off neckline st. Pin the left front to the neckline. Lay the Right side of the collar over the Left across the bound off sts of the neckline, lining up the collar BO with the last bound off neckline st in that direction. Pin in place.

With a tapestry needle, whipstitch the collar to the neckline through all three layers, beginning in the center of the neckline and working up each side to the first picked up sts.

Collar Ribbing
With smaller needles and starting at the back neck, pick up collar sts: PU and K 32 (32, 34, 36, 36, 42, 42, 44, 46) sts across the back neck, 30 (30, 32, 32, 34, 34, 36, 36, 36) sts to the bound off sts at the center neck, 16 (16, 18, 18, 18, 20, 20, 22, 22) sts across the bound off neck sts, and 30 (30, 32, 32, 34, 34, 36, 36, 36) sts to the back. 108 (108, 116, 118, 122, 130, 134, 138, 140) sts total. PM and join to work in the round.

Work in K1, P1 rib for 2". BO all sts loosely, and break yarn leaving 36" tail. Turn the sweater inside-out. Fold the collar ribbing in towards the picked-up edge. Using the yarn tail, whipstitch the bound-off edge to the inside of the picked-up edge.

Finishing
Weave in ends, wash and block.

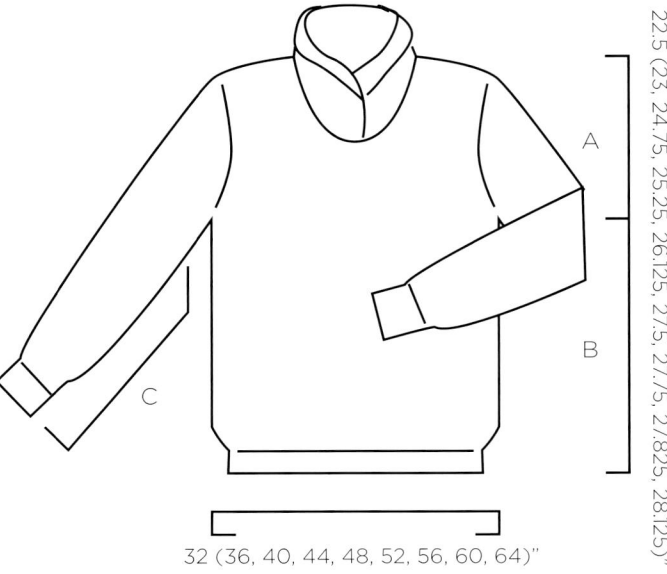

32 (36, 40, 44, 48, 52, 56, 60, 64)"

A 7 (7.5, 8.25, 8.625, 9, 10.5, 10.75, 10.825, 11.125)"
B 15.5 (15.5, 16.5, 16.625, 17.125, 17, 17, 17, 17)"
C 17.5 (17.5, 18, 18, 18, 18.5, 19, 19, 18.5)"

22.5 (23, 24.75, 25.25, 26.125, 27.5, 27.75, 27.825, 28.125)"

CIRCLET CARDIGAN
by Kerin Dimeler-Laurence

Finished Measurements
32 (36, 40, 44, 48, 52, 56, 60, 64)" finished bust measurement

Yarn
Knit Picks Gloss DK (70% Merino wool, 30% Silk; 123 yards/50g): Clover 25591, 14 (16, 18, 20, 21, 22, 24, 26, 27) balls.

Needles
US 6 (4mm) straight or 32-60" circular needles, plus DPNs or longer circulars for Magic Loop, or size to obtain gauge, and spare needles in same size

Circular needles and DPNs or longer circulars for Magic Loop one size smaller than those used to obtain gauge

Notions
Yarn Needle
Stitch Markers
Scrap Yarn or stitch holders
Cable Needle
10 (10, 10, 11, 11, 11, 12, 12, 13) .75" buttons

Gauge
26 sts and 32 rows = 4" in Staghorn (body) cable, blocked.
22 sts and 32 rows = 4" in St st, blocked.

Circlet Cardigan

Notes:
All references to Right and Left are as worn.

Wrap and Turn:
Work until the stitch to be wrapped. If knitting: bring yarn to the front of the work, slip next st as if to purl, return the yarn to the back; turn work and slip wrapped st onto RH needle. Continue across row. If purling: bring yarn to the back of the work, slip next st as if to purl, return the yarn to the front; turn work and slip wrapped st onto RH needle. Continue across row.

Picking up wraps: Work to the wrapped st. If knitting, insert the RH needle under the wrap(s), then through the wrapped st K-wise. Knit the wrap(s) together with the wrapped st. If Purling, slip the wrapped st P-wise onto the RH needle, and use the LH needle to lift the wrap(s) and place them on the RH needle. Slip wrap(s) and unworked st back to LH needle; purl all together through the back loop.

M1R (Make 1 Right-leaning stitch)
PU the bar between st just worked and next st and place on LH needle backwards (incorrect stitch mount). Knit through the front loop.

For video and photo tutorials for these and other techniques such as the Mattress stitch, grafting methods and other techniques, visit the Knit Picks website at http://www.knitpicks.com/tutorials.

DIRECTIONS

The body of this sweater is subtly decreased to the point where it is joined with the sleeves. The yoke is knit sideways, using short rows to shape the neckline.

Sleeves

The sleeves begin with a narrow turned hem. The sleeves are identical and worked separately until the armscyes; they are then joined with the body and worked together in the round

With smaller needles, CO 48 (48, 52, 56, 58, 63, 66, 67, 72) sts. PM and join to work in the round, being careful not to twist sts. Knit five rounds. Purl a turning round.

On the next round, switch to larger needles and begin working from the Sleeve chart for your size. Work a KFB increase at the beginning and end of every 6th (6th, 6th and 13th, 5th, 5th, 5th, 5th, 4th, 4th) round 21 (21, 11, 28, 27, 28, 27, 34, 36) times. Work 14 (14, 1, 4, 9, 4, 13, 12, 8) rounds in pattern. After all increases have been worked, 90 (90, 96, 112, 112, 119, 120, 135, 144) sts are on the needles. After the last round of the chart, place sleeve on stitch holder or scrap yarn.

Complete second sleeve to this point.

Body

Like the sleeves, the body begins with a narrow turned hem. It is worked flat with a narrow button band up each front edge. It is joined and worked with the sleeves for a short section before the yoke begins.

All shaping in the Body occurs between the pattern repeats. The decreases in these spaces are spread out to give an A-line shape.

With smaller needles, CO 242 (275, 292, 328, 364, 385, 411, 446, 472) sts. Work in St st for five rows. Knit a turning row.

On the next row, switch to larger needles and begin working the Body in pattern. Between each pattern repeat are columns of purl sts, in which the Body's shaping is concealed.

Sizes 32 (44, 60, 64): Purl 2 selvedge sts, then work across first section of Body Repeat chart.

All sizes: *(P 3 (3, 4, 4, 4, 5, 3, 3, 4), work Center section of Body Repeat chart); repeat from * 13 (16, 16, 17, 20, 20, 24, 25, 25) times, (P 3 (3, 4, 4, 4, 5, 3, 3, 4).
Sizes 32 (44, 60, 64): Work across last section of Body Repeat chart, Purl 2 selvedge sts.

Continue working flat in pattern as established for a total of 20 rows (five vertical pattern repeats), placing markers as called for on the Body Repeat chart.

From this point, decreases will steadily remove one stitch from each pattern repeat until there are 15 (15, 16, 16, 16, 17, 15, 15, 16) sts across each repeat of Purl sts and Pattern. To work decreases, on the first row of the next 4-row repeat *work a P2tog decrease to the right of the first cable section, then every fourth repeat of the cable section after that (e.g., first; fifth, ninth, thirteenth repeats of the cable section after that); sizes 36, 40, 48, 52, 56: P2tog in the purl section after the last repeat. Complete the current 4-row repeat, then work two more 4-row repeats. 4 (5, 5, 5, 6, 6, 7, 7, 7) sts removed. On the first row of the following 4-row repeat, work this decrease on the second cable pattern repeat, then every fourth after that (e.g. second, sixth, tenth, fourteenth repeats of the cable section after that); sizes 32, 44, 60, 64: P2tog in the purl section after the last repeat. Complete the current 4-row repeat, then work two more 4-row repeats. 3 (4, 4, 4, 5, 5, 6, 6, 6) sts removed. On the first row of the following 4-row repeat, work this decrease on the third cable pattern repeat, then every fourth repeat of the cable section. Complete the current 4-row repeat, then work two more 4-row repeats. 3 (4, 4, 4, 5, 5, 6, 6, 6) sts removed. On the first row of the following 4-row repeat, work this decrease on the fourth cable pattern repeat, then every fourth repeat of the cable section. Complete the current 4-row repeat.* Work two more 4-row repeats. 3 (4, 4, 4, 5, 5, 6, 6, 6) sts removed. Repeat between *s once more. Continue in cable pattern for 3 (4, 4, 5, 5, 6, 7, 7, 7) repeats [12 (16, 16, 20, 20, 24, 28, 28, 28) rows]. 214 (241, 258, 292, 322, 343, 361, 394, 420) sts.

Attach Sleeves

On the next row, the sleeves are attached to the body and all are worked together until the yoke.

Work across the front right of the Body from row 1 of the Body Repeat chart to 8 sts before right underarm marker. *Place the next 15 (15, 16, 16, 16, 17, 15, 15, 16) sts on a stitch holder or scrap yarn. Place a Sleeve on spare needles, keeping the first 8 and last 7 (7, 8, 8, 8, 9, 7, 7, 8) live sts on scrap yarn or stitch holder. Knit directly from the last knit st of the Body around the Sleeve in pattern to the last live st. Knit directly from the Sleeve onto the next live st of the Body*, and continue in pattern across Back to 7 sts before left underarm marker. Repeat between *s and continue in pattern to the end of the row.

Continue working in pattern across all 334 (361, 386, 452, 482, 513, 541, 604, 644) sts for 7 (7, 7, 11, 11, 11, 15, 15, 15) rows. BO all sts loosely.

Yoke

The Yoke is worked sideways separately and then sewn on to the cardigan body. With larger needles CO 45 (47, 49, 52, 54, 58, 68, 70, 71) sts, and begin working from Yoke chart, following the instructions given with the chart.

After Yoke has been knit, line up the long edge of the Yoke with the bound off edge of the Body. Pin in place, and sew the Yoke to the Body using Mattress stitch.

Neck edge and Button Bands

Sts are picked up around the neck edge and along the front of the cardigan opening to create the front bands.

Neckline

With RS facing and starting at the right front neck edge, with larger needles PU and knit 66 (66, 70, 78, 84, 84, 88, 84) sts around the neckline. Work in Garter st (K every row) for 7 rows. BO all sts loosely.

Button Band

With RS facing, with larger needles PU and K 137 (142, 144, 150, 151, 157, 171, 173, 177) sts along the Right front edge of the cardigan. Work in Garter st (K every row) for 7 rows. BO all sts loosely.

Buttonhole Band

With RS facing, with larger needles PU and K 137 (142, 144, 150, 151, 157, 171, 173, 177) sts along the Left front edge of the cardigan. Knit 3 rows. On the next (WS) row, K5 (7, 8, 3, 5, 8, 8, 7, 3), *K2tog, YO twice, SSK, K10*; repeat between *s 9 (9, 9, 10, 10, 10, 11, 11, 12) times, K2tog, YO twice, SSK, K to end. Knit the next row, working (K1, K1 TBL) over each double YO. K 2 rows. BO all sts loosely.

Finishing

Turn cardigan inside out. Fold hem facings inside along turning rows. Whipstitch the edges to the WS of the cardigan, making sure stitches don't show on the RS.

Graft live sts at the underarms and weave in all ends. Wash and block to measurements. Sew buttons opposite buttonholes.

Legend

- **knit** — RS knit, WS purl
- **purl** — RS purl, WS knit
- **c1 over 2 right P** — sl2 to CN, hold in back. k1, p2 from CN
- **Left Twist, purl bg** — sl1 to CN, hold in front. p1. k1 from CN
- **Right Twist, purl bg** — sl1 to CN, hold in back. k1, p1 from CN
- **c1 over 2 left P** — sl 1 to CN, hold in front. p2, k1 from CN
- **Right Twist** — Skip the first stitch, knit into 2nd stitch, then knit skipped stitch. Slip both stitches from needle tog OR k2tog leaving sts on LH needle, then k first st again, sl both sts off needle.
- **c3 over 2 right P** — sl2 to CN, hold in back. k3, then p2 from CN
- **c3 over 1 left P** — sl3 to CN, hold in front. p1, k3 from CN
- **c3 over 3 right P** — sl3 to CN, hold in back. k3 then p3 from CN
- **c3 over 1 right P** — sl1 to CN, hold in back. k3, p1 from CN
- **c3 over 3 right** — sl3 to CN, hold in back. k3, then k3 from CN
- **c3 over 2 left P** — sl3 to CN, hold in front. p2, then k3 from CN
- **c3 over 3 left** — sl3 to CN, hold in front. k3, k3 from CN
- **c3 over 3 left P** — sl3 to CN, hold in front. p3, k3 from CN

Body Repeat (Staghorn Pattern)

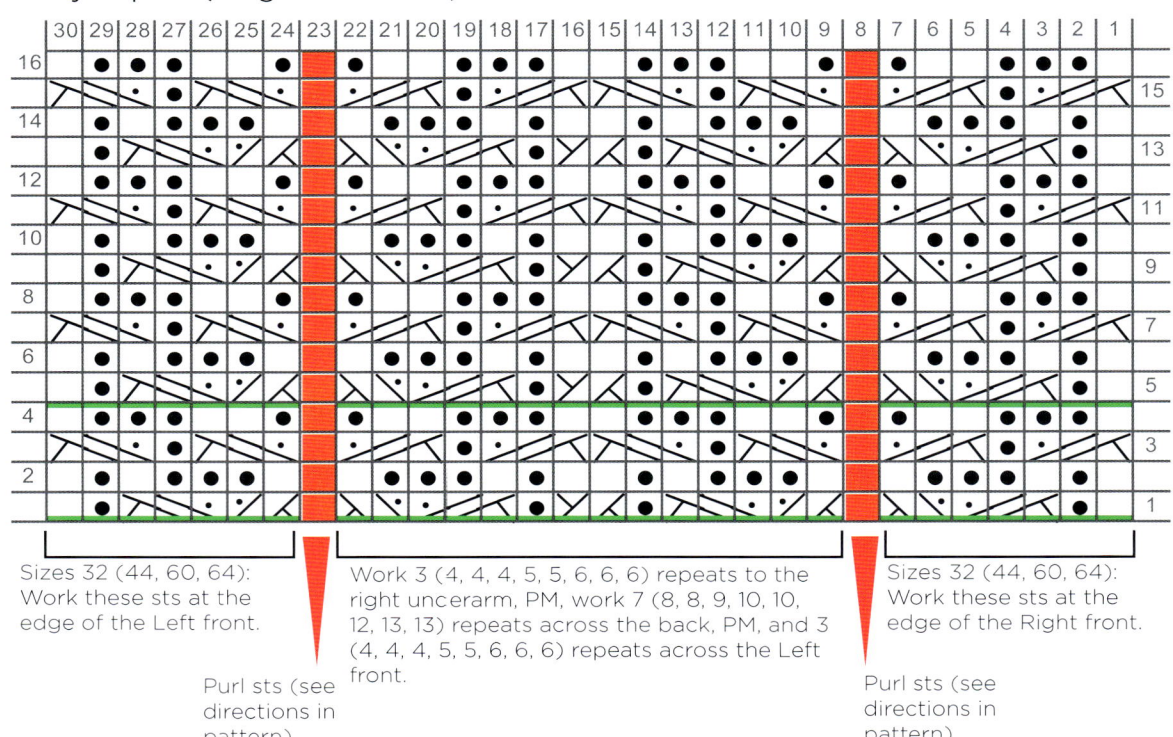

Sizes 32 (44, 60, 64): Work these sts at the edge of the Left front.

Work 3 (4, 4, 4, 5, 5, 6, 6, 6) repeats to the right underarm, PM, work 7 (8, 8, 9, 10, 10, 12, 13, 13) repeats across the back, PM, and 3 (4, 4, 4, 5, 5, 6, 6, 6) repeats across the Left front.

Purl sts (see directions in pattern)

Sizes 32 (44, 60, 64): Work these sts at the edge of the Right front.

Purl sts (see directions in pattern)

Read RS (odd numbered) rows from right to left and WS (even numbered) rows from left to right.

Note: The pattern is 4 rows; extra repeats are shown for ease of visualization.

Circlet Cardigan

Sleeves (Staghorn Pattern)

Sizes 32, 36, 56, 60: 15 st repeat

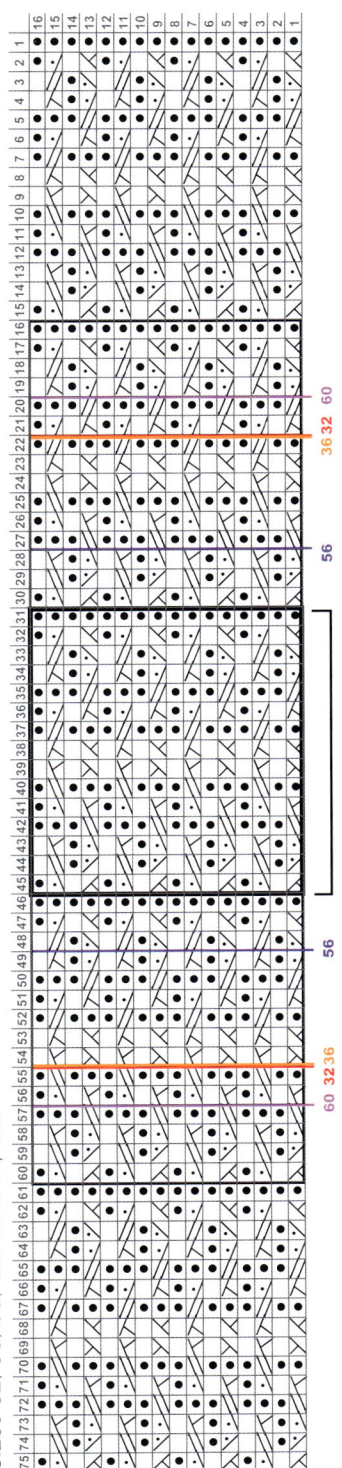

Repeat these 15 sts 2 (2, 4, 3) times

Sizes 40, 44, 48, 64: 16 st repeat

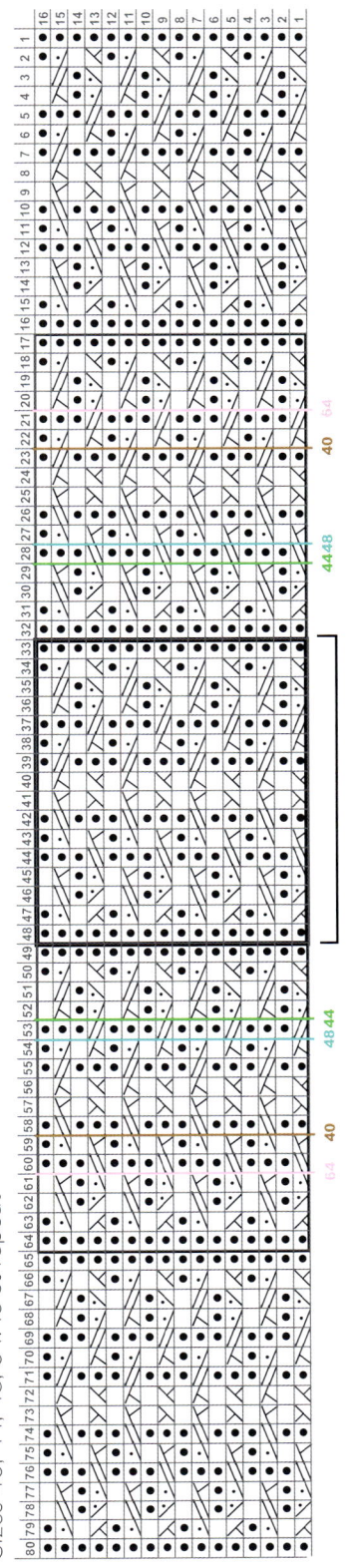

Repeat these 16 sts 2 (3, 3, 3) times

Size 52: 17 st repeat

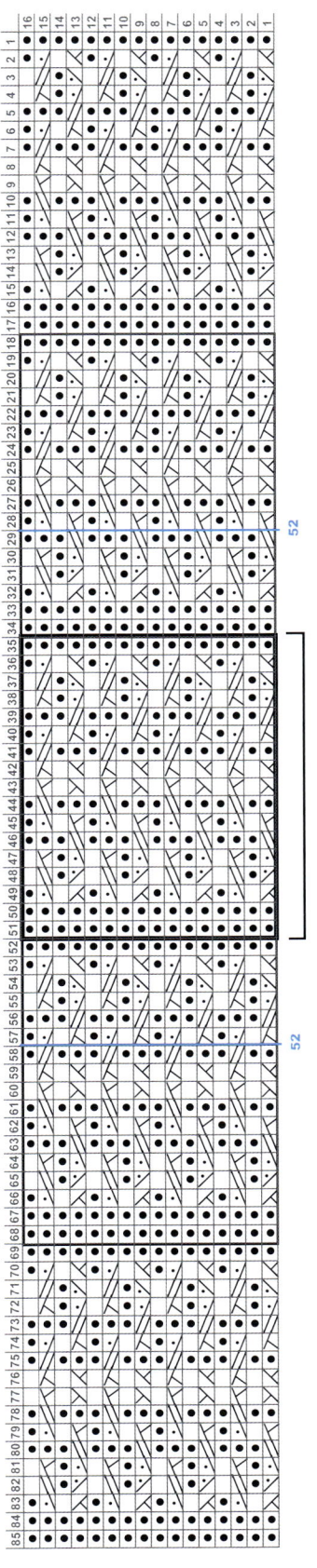

Repeat these 17 sts 3 times

All rounds are read right to left. The pattern is 4 rows; extra repeats are shown for ease of visualization. Size lines indicate the stitches at cast on; work increases beyond these lines. When all increases are completed, there will be even repeats of the pattern. Follow increase instructions in written pattern.

Work increases as a KFB in the first and last stitches; work all other stitches as shown. As you increase through cables, only work those cables that have enough stitches to complete the whole cable. Otherwise, knit the sts that would be knit and purl those that would be purled in the cable.

Circlet Cardigan | 33

Yoke

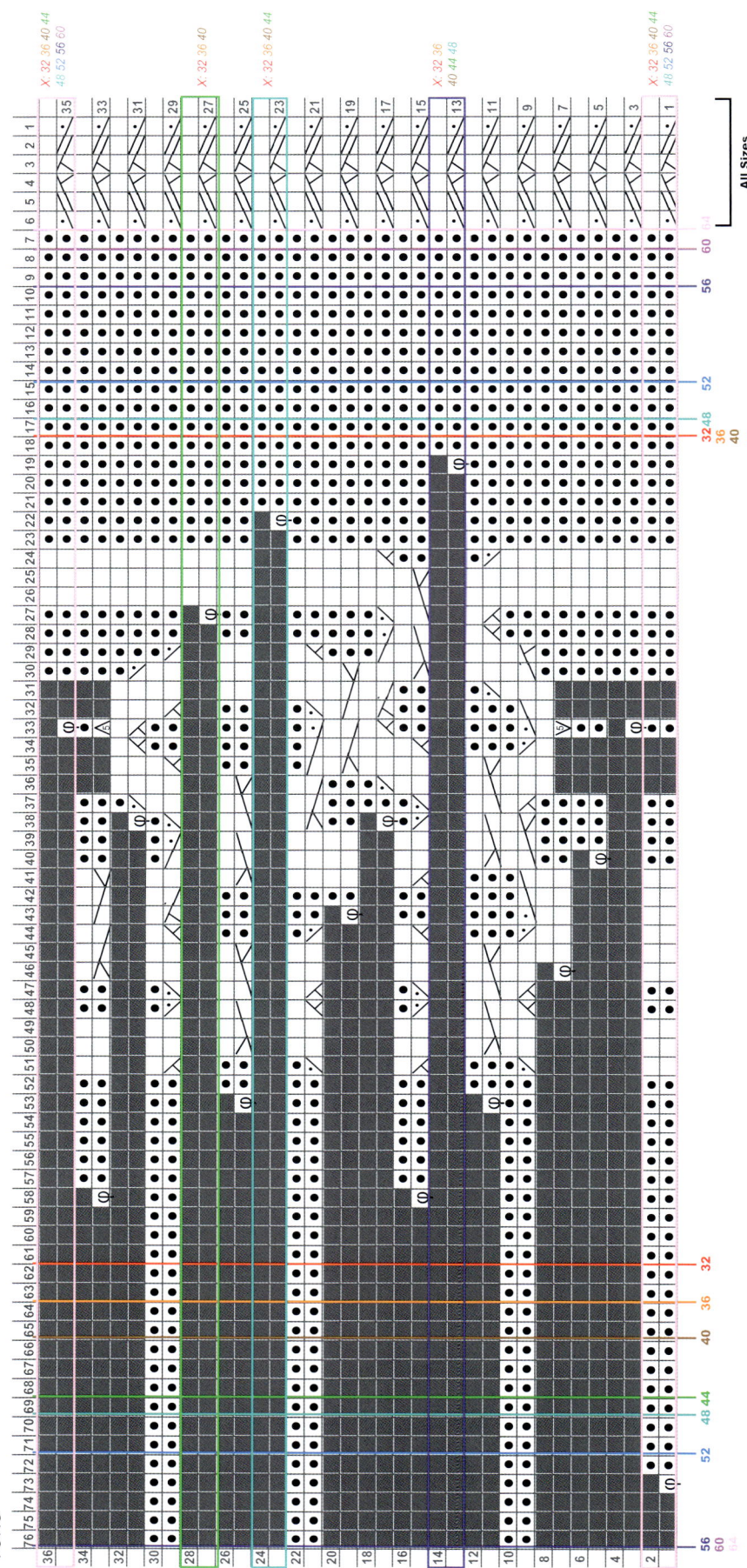

Follow the chart from bottom to top. RS (odd numbered) rows are read from right to left, and WS rows from left to right.

The Yoke chart represents all sizes. Only size 64 will work all 36 rows and 76 sts of the repeat; all other sizes have a number of rows and stitches excluded to shorten the height and width of the yoke. All sizes work the first 6 sts; then skip to the first stitch noted for your size, ending the row at the last stitch noted for your size. Skip rows noted with "X: your size", and move on to the next row.

Repeat this chart 16 (16, 17, 19, 19, 20, 20, 21, 20) times, avoiding rows noted for your size.

After the last row, BO all sts. Continue from written pattern.

Wrap & Turn
See instructions in Notes section of pattern.

No Stitch
Placeholder - No stitch made.

increase 5
M1, KFB twice into stitch, M1: 5 sts increased.

decrease 5
Sl 4 sts to RH needle. *Pass 2nd st on RHN over the first (center)st, then pass this center st back to LHN. Pass 2nd st on LHN over the center st. Pass center st back to RHN* and repeat between *'s once more; pass 2nd st on RHN over center st. Leave st on RHN.

34 | Circlet Cardigan

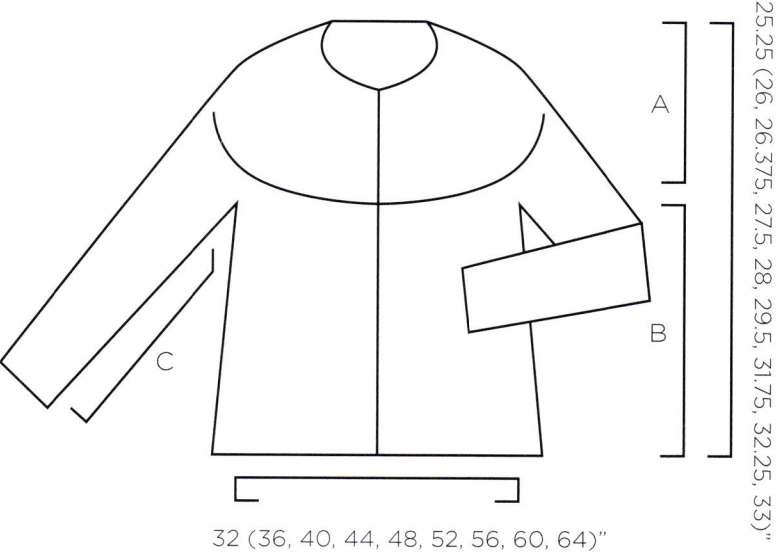

32 (36, 40, 44, 48, 52, 56, 60, 64)"

A   8.25 (8.5, 8.875, 9.5, 9.875, 10.625, 12.375, 12.75, 12.875)"

B   16 (16.5, 16.5, 17, 17, 17.5, 18, 18, 18.5)"

C   17.5 (17.5, 18, 18, 18, 18, 18.5, 18.5, 18)"

GLASS KNOT AFGHAN
by Kerin Dimeler-Laurence

Finished Measurements
Lap Blanket: 34x45"
Throw: 45x56"
Bedspread: 68x79"

Yarn
Knit Picks Chroma Worsted (70% Wool, 30% Nylon; 198 yards/100g):
CC Impressionist 25870, 4 (6, 12) balls.
Knit Picks Wool of the Andes Worsted (100% Peruvian Highland Wool; 110 yards/50g): MC Bittersweet Heather 24652, 10 (14, 30) balls.

Needles
US 7 (4.5mm) DPNs or long circular needles for Magic Loop, or size to obtain gauge
DPNs in same size to work I-cord

Notions
Yarn Needle
Stitch Markers

Gauge
21 sts and 21 rows = 4" in stranded St st in the round, blocked.

Glass Knot Afghan

Notes:
Celtic knots glow like stained glass in this clever afghan. Each of the three sizes of afghan is made of several tiles that are knit identically and sewn together. What really gives these blankets their glow is the subtle shading of Chroma, which makes each tile unique.

There are three types of tile: Full Tiles (the squares), Half Tiles, and Quarter Tiles. The Full Tiles are worked in the round, and the others are worked flat. This will require stranding from the WS. In each case, the cast-on row forms a selvedge for seaming.

To ensure that the blanket lies flat, block each tile to the proper dimensions before seaming.

For video and photo tutorials for techniques such as Applied I-cord, visit the Knit Picks website at www.knitpicks.com/tutorials.

DIRECTIONS
Full Tiles
With MC, CO 172 sts, placing markers after every 43 sts. PM and join to work in the round. Begin working from round 1 of Knot Chart, repeating the chart between markers (four times around). After the last round, 4 sts remain. Break MC and CC, and using a yarn needle, pass the MC tail through the remaining live sts; pull tight to close the hole. Weave in ends. Repeat these directions for each Full Tile.

Half Tiles
With MC, CO 86 sts, placing marker after 43 sts. Begin working from row 1 of Knot Chart (RS), repeating the chart twice across. After the last row, 2 sts remain. Knit these two sts together. Break MC and CC, and using a yarn needle, pass the MC tail through the remaining live st; pull tight to bind off. Weave in ends. Repeat these directions for each Half Tile.

Quarter Tiles
With MC, CO 43 sts. Begin working from row 1 of Knot Chart (RS). After the last row, 1 st remains. Break MC and CC, and using a yarn needle, pass the MC tail through the remaining live st; pull tight to bind off. Weave in ends. Repeat these directions for each Quarter Tile.

Finishing
Block each tile to the proper dimensions. When fully dry, begin seaming the tiles together with MC and using Mattress Stitch; it is easiest to sew them in strips, and then sew the strips together.

Border
A decorative I-cord border finishes off the afghan. Hold the afghan with RS facing, and beginning at one corner, work from Applied I-Cord directions around the outside of the afghan.

Applied I-Cord
With MC and using DPNs, CO 3 sts.
*Knit two stitches and slip the third stitch knitwise.
PU and knit a stitch from the edge of the adghan. You will now have 4 stitches on your right needle.
Use your left needle tip to pass the slipped stitch over the last knitted stitch. This will leave you with three stitches on your right needle.
Slip these three stitches back onto the left needle tip, or slide to the other end of the needle, purlwise. Tug on the working yarn to tighten up the stitches.
Repeat these steps from *.

After the I-cord has been worked around the entire afghan edge, break yarn. Using a yarn needle, graft the live stitches at the end of the I-cord to the cast-on edge of the I-cord.

Weave in ends, wash, and block.

Knot Chart

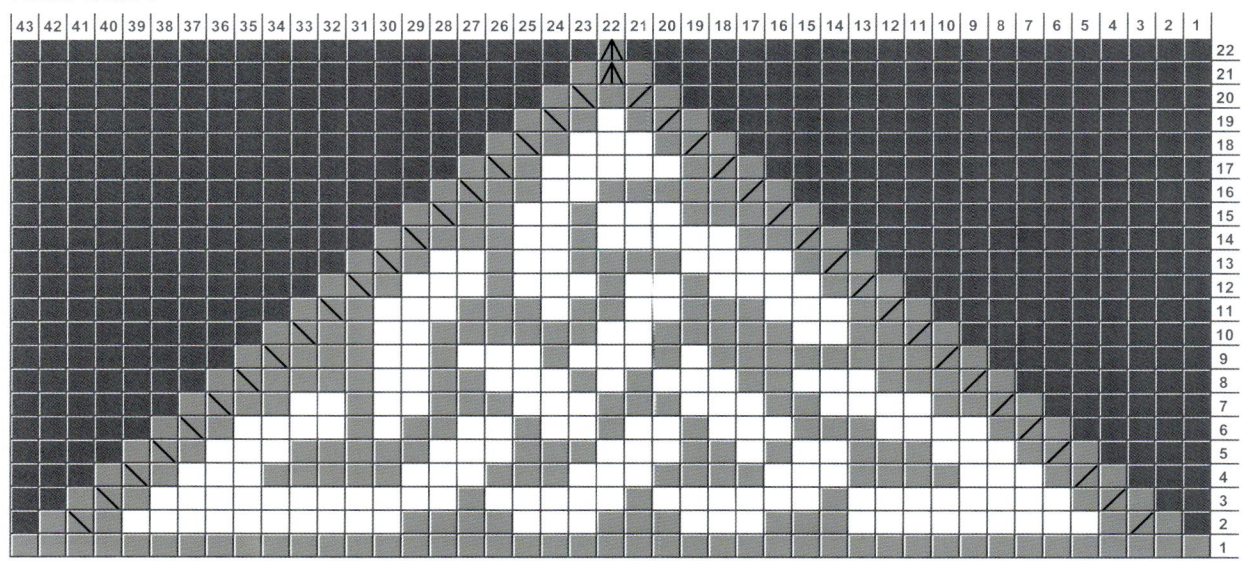

The chart is followed from bottom to top. When knitting in the round, read each row from right to left as a RS round. For knitting flat, read RS rows from right to left, and WS rows from left to right.

Afghan Layouts

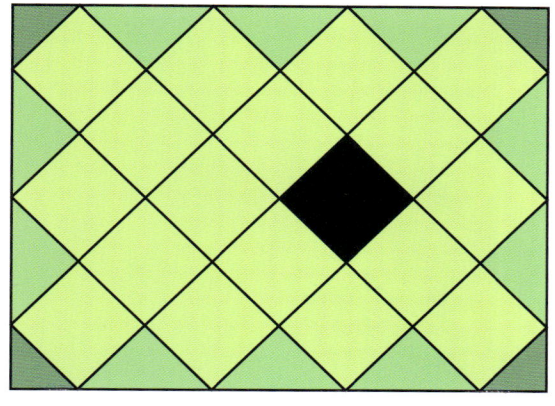

Lap Blanket

18 Full Tiles
10 Half-tiles
4 Quarter Tiles

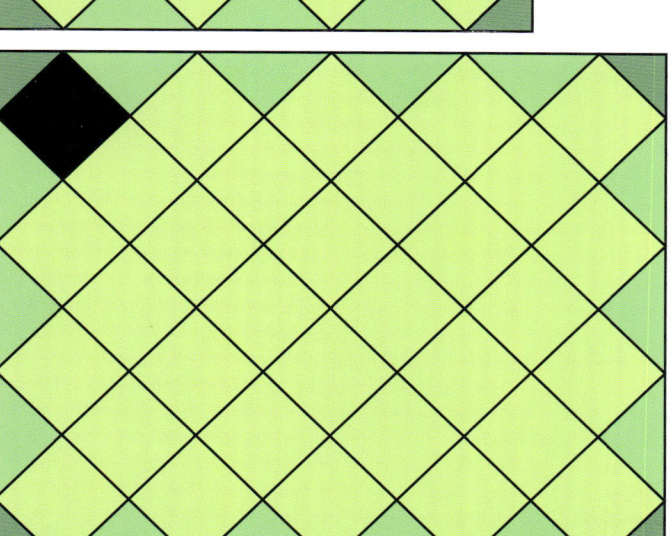

Throw

32 Full Tiles
14 Half-tiles
4 Quarter Tiles

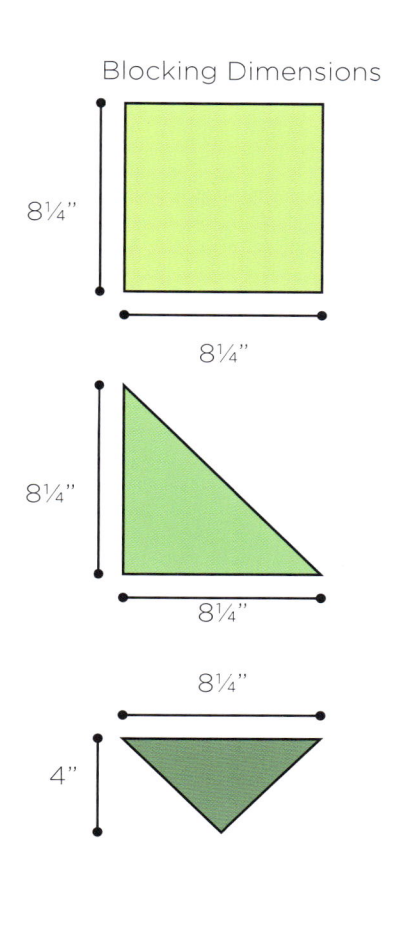

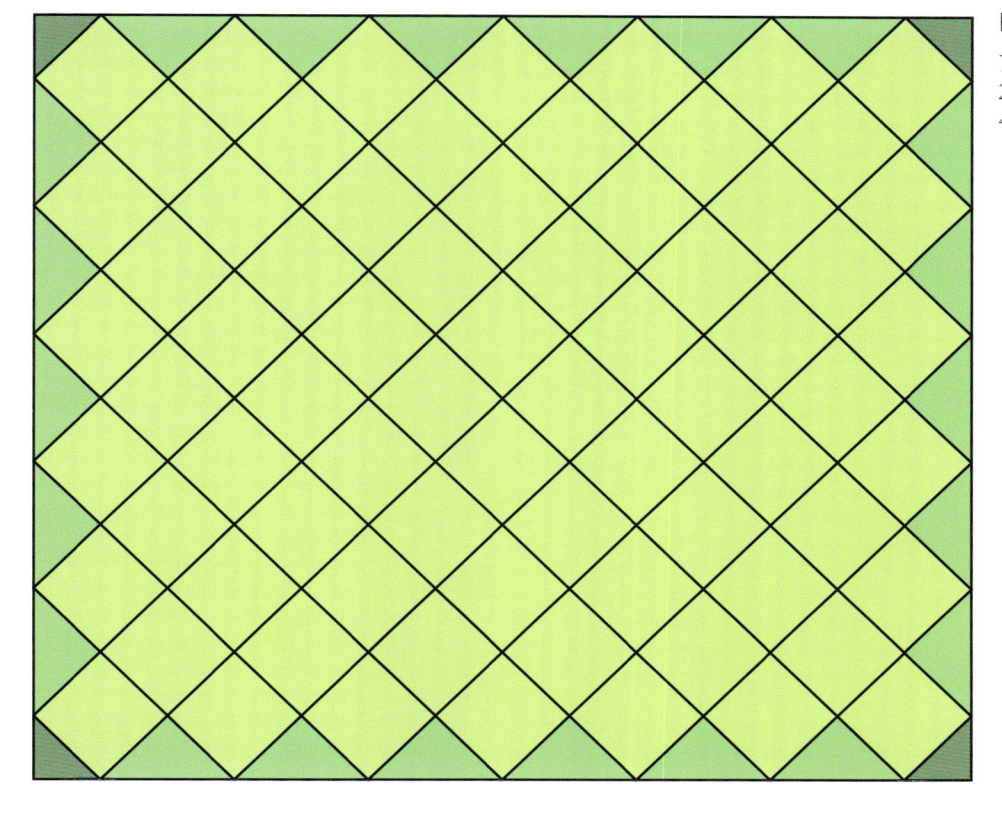

Bedspread

72 Full Tiles
22 Half-tiles
4 Quarter Tiles

Blocking Dimensions

8¼"
8¼"

8¼"
8¼"

8¼"
4"

Glass Knot Afghan | 39

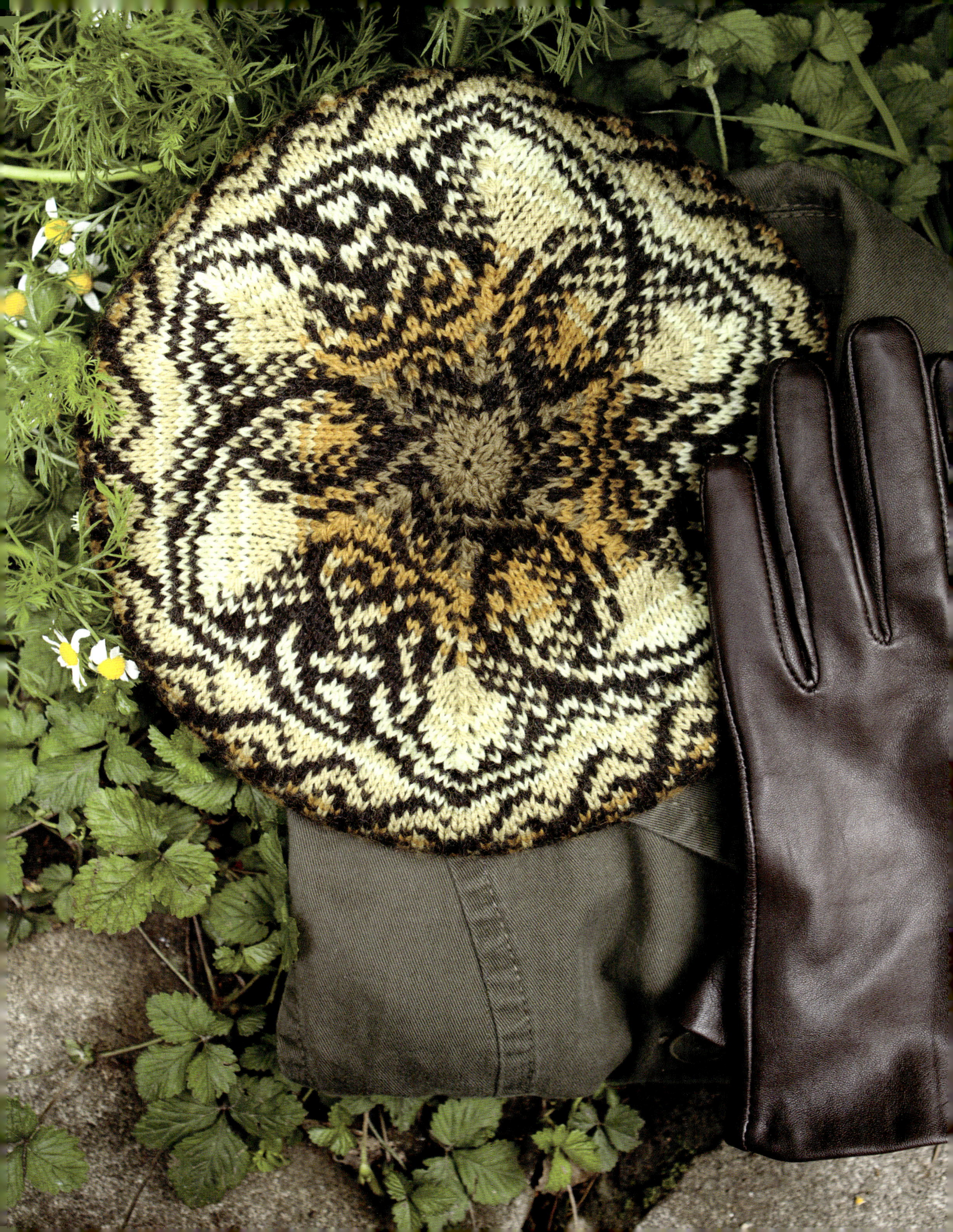

MONUMENT TAM

by Kerin Dimeler-Laurence

FINISHED MEASUREMENTS
11" diameter

YARN
Knit Picks *Palette* (100% Peruvian Highland Wool; 231 yards/50g): MC Bittersweet Heather 24239; CC1 Caper 25545, CC2 Serpentine 25100, CC3 Lichen 26047, CC4 Green Tea Heather 24258, 1 ball each.

NEEDLES
US 2 (2.75 mm) DPNs plus 16" circular needles if desired, or 40" or longer circulars for Magic Loop, or size to obtain gauge

NOTIONS
Yarn Needle
Stitch Markers
11" Dinner Plate or other flat, round object for blocking.

GAUGE
32 sts and 32 rows = 4" in stranded St st in the round, blocked.

Monument Tam

Notes:

M1L (Make 1 Left-leaning stitch): PU the bar between st just worked and next st and place on LH needle as a regular stitch; knit through the back of the loop.

DIRECTIONS

A band of corrugated ribbing begins this tam, which is patterned to resemble carved stone.

With MC and smaller needles, loosely CO 144 sts. PM and join to work in the round, being careful not to twist sts.

Work one round in K2, P2 rib.

Corrugated Ribbing

On the next round, attach CC4 and begin working in corrugated rib: *K2 in MC, P2 in CC*; repeat between *s around hat. Work a total of 16 rounds in corrugated ribbing, changing CCs as follows:

2 rounds CC4
2 rounds CC3
2 rounds CC2
4 rounds CC1
2 rounds CC2
2 rounds CC3
2 rounds CC4

After the last round of Corrugated Ribbing, break CC4 and work one round in K2, P2 rib in MC.

Increasing for Crown

On the next round, stitches are added to bring the stitch count to the full number needed to work the charts.

(K3, M1L) around: 48 sts added, 192 sts total. Switch to larger needles; without breaking MC, attach CC1 and knit one round.

Crown

Begin working from the Crown chart around the hat. Repeat these 64 sts three times around the hat, changing colors as shown in the chart. Switch to DPNs when too few sts remain for circular needles.

After the last round, 6 sts remain. Break yarn. With yarn needle, pass the tail of CC1 through the remaining live sts; pull tight to close the hole.

Finishing

Weave in ends.

Wash the tam. Block over an 11" dinner plate, with the crown of the tam across the underside of the plate. Allow the tam to try fully before removing from the plate.

Crown

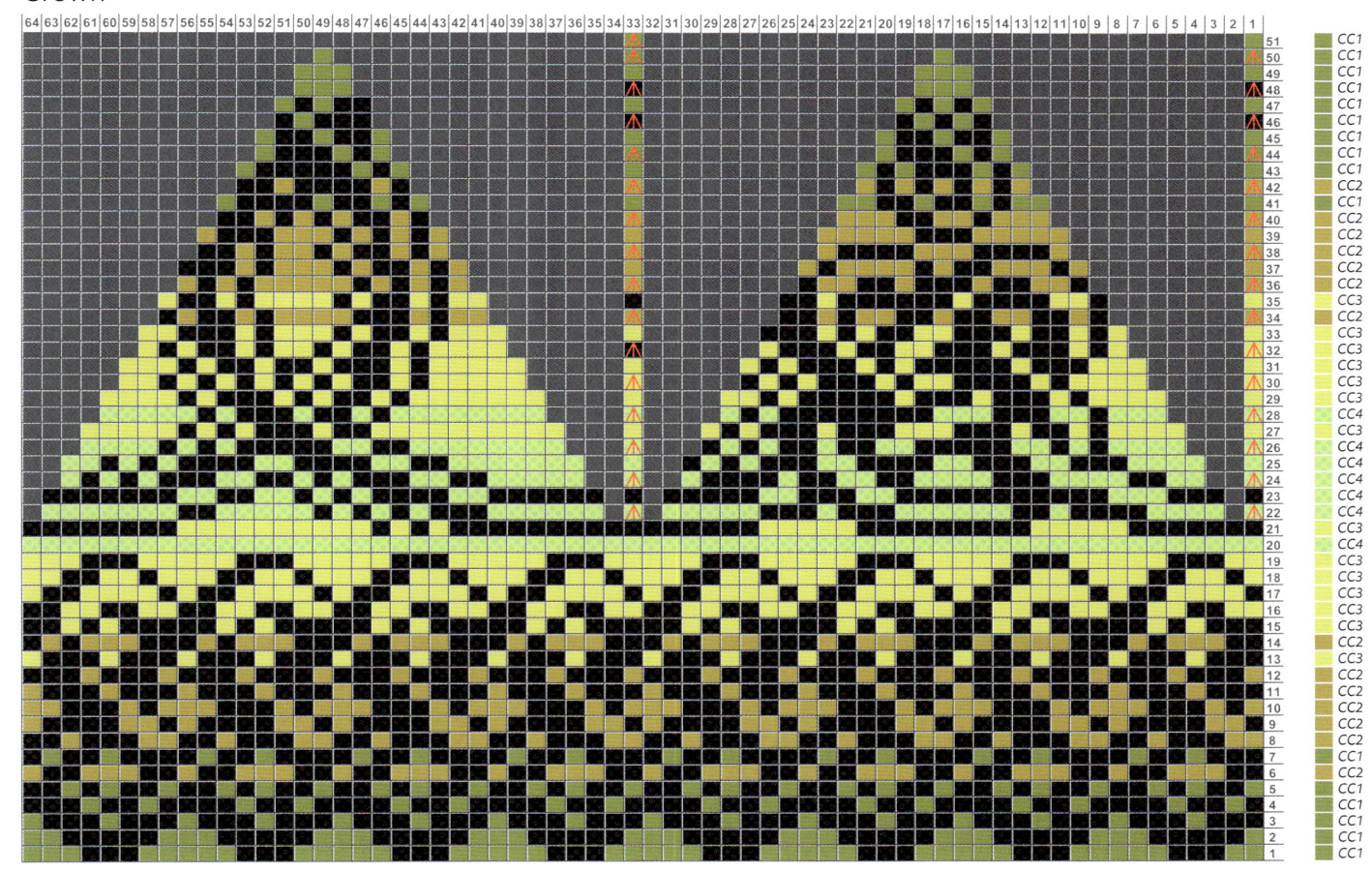

Chart is read from bottom to top. All rounds are read right to left. Repeat chart 3 times around tam.

- ■ **MC**
- ▓ **No Stitch**
- ☐ **Knit**
- ⋏ **Centered Double Decrease (CDD)**
  Slip two stitches to the RH needle knit-wise. Knit the next stitch, then pass two slipped sts over; two sts removed.

Note on crown decreases: On the first repeat of each round, work an SSK as the first decrease on even-numbered rounds. Slip the last stitch of the round (the one that will be decreased) to the beginning of the following round, and K2tog with the first stitch of this next (odd-numbered) round. This splits the CDD over the beginning and end of round

Monument Tam | 43

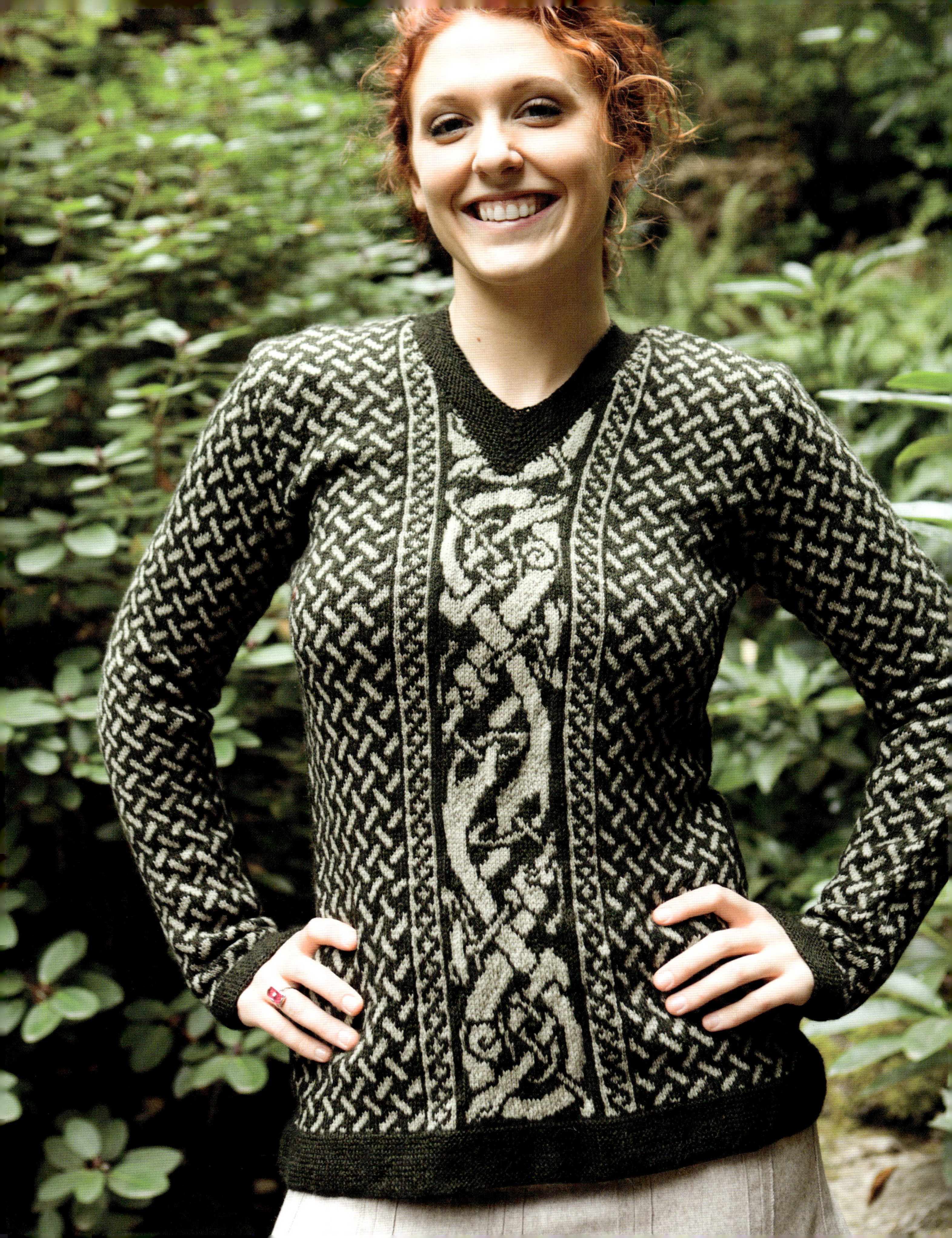

FIA PULLOVER
by Kerin Dimeler-Laurence

Finished Measurements
To fit 32 (36, 40, 44, 48, 52, 56, 60, 64)" bust measurement, worn with about 2" of positive ease. Finished bust measurement: 34 (38, 41.5, 45.5, 49.5, 54.5, 58, 62, 65.5)"

Yarn
Knit Picks Palette (100% Peruvian Highland Wool; 231 yards/50g): MC Larch Heather 25543, 5 (6, 6, 7, 7, 8, 9, 10, 10,) balls, CC Sea Grass 26049, 4 (4, 4, 5, 5, 6, 7, 8, 9) balls.

Needles
US 3 (3.25mm) 32" circular needles, plus DPNs or longer circulars for Magic Loop method, or size to obtain gauge
32" circular needles one size smaller than those to obtain gauge, plus DPNs or longer circulars for Magic Loop method

Notions
Yarn Needle
Stitch Markers
Scrap yarn or stitch holders
Spare Needles
Sewing needle and thread for steeks

Gauge
32 sts and 38 rows = 4" in stranded St st in the round, blocked.

Fia Pullover

Notes:
All references to Right and Left are as worn. Splice yarn ends together where possible; this will save time in finishing.

M1L (Make 1 Left-leaning stitch): PU the bar between st just worked and next st and place on LH needle mounted as a regular knit stitch; knit through the back of the loop.

M1R (Make 1 Right-leaning stitch): PU the bar between st just worked and next st and place on LH needle backwards (incorrect stitch mount). Knit through the front of the loop.

Wrap and Turn (W&T)
Work until the stitch to be wrapped. If knitting: bring yarn to the front of the work, slip next st as if to purl, return the yarn to the back; turn work and slip wrapped st onto RH needle. Continue across row. If purling: bring yarn to the back of the work, slip next st as if to purl, return the yarn to the front; turn work and slip wrapped st onto RH needle. Continue across row.

Picking up wraps: Work to the wrapped st. If knitting, insert the RH needle under the wrap(s), then through the wrapped st K-wise. Knit the wrap(s) together with the wrapped st. If Purling, slip the wrapped st P-wise onto the RH needle, and use the LH needle to lift the wrap(s) and place them on the RH needle. Slip wrap(s) and unworked st back to LH needle; purl all together through the back loop.

Three-needle Bind Off (3-needle BO)
Hold the two pieces of knitting together with the points facing to the right. Insert a *third* needle into the first stitch on each of the needles knitwise, starting with the front needle. Work a knit stitch, pulling the loop through both of the stitches you've inserted the third needle through. After you've pulled the loop through, slip the first stitch off of each of the needles. This takes two stitches (one from the front needle and one from the back) and joins them to make one finished stitch on the third needle (held in your right hand). Repeat this motion, inserting your needle into one stitch on the front and back needles, knitting them together and slipping them off of the needles. Each time you complete a second stitch, pass the first finished stitch over the second and off of the needle (as you would in a traditional bind-off).

DIRECTIONS
Sleeves

The sleeves begin with a simple Garter stitch cuff. The sleeves are identical and worked separately in Lattice pattern until the sleeve cap; they are then joined with steeks and worked together in the round to the top of the caps.

With smaller needles and MC, CO 68 (70, 74, 82, 86, 96, 100, 104, 108). PM and join to work in the round, being careful not to twist sts. Knit in Garter st (Knit one round, Purl one round) for 1.5", ending having worked a knit round.

Switch to larger needles. K1 in MC, attach CC and begin working from Sleeve chart to the last st, following repeat directions for your size; K1 in MC. These two sts in MC will continue to run up the underside of the arm and are not shown in the chart. At the same time, work Sleeve increases.

Sleeve Increase Round: K1 in MC, M1L in pattern, work from Sleeve chart to last st, M1R in pattern, K1 in MC. 2 sts increased.

Sizes 44, 48, 60: work a Sleeve Increase Round on the first round.

All sizes: Work a Sleeve Increase Round every 8th (6th, 6th, 5th & 11th, 5th, 4th, 4th, 3rd & 7th, 3rd) round 19 (25, 26, 14, 33, 39, 42, 23, 51) times.

All sizes: Work 9 (11, 7, 10, 1, 10, 0, 7, 13) rounds in pattern. There are now 106 (120, 126, 140, 154, 174, 184, 198, 210) sts on the needles. You should have just completed the last round of the last repeat of the sleeve chart. Work second sleeve to this point.

Sleeve Cap

On the first round of the Sleeve Cap, stitches are bound off at the armscye of one sleeve and then the next; the sleeves are joined with a steek and continued in the round.

Work across the first round of the Sleeve Cap to the last 5 (6, 7, 6, 6, 5, 5, 5, 5) sts. BO the last 4 (5, 6, 5, 5, 4, 4, 4, 4) charted sts and the last MC st of the round, then BO the first MC st of the next round and 4 (5, 6, 5, 5, 4, 4, 4, 4) sts of the second round of the Sleeve Cap. Continue to the end of the second round of the Sleeve Cap. 96 (108, 112, 128, 142, 164, 174, 188, 200) sts. After the last live st for your size, place sleeve on scrap yarn or stitch holder, and work second sleeve to this point.

When both sleeves are worked through the Armscye bind-off round, place first sleeve back on a set of spare needles. Directly after the last st of the second sleeve, PM and CO 7 sts in alternating colors. PM and begin knitting from the next round of the chart across the first sleeve; this joins the two together at one side. After completing this round on the first sleeve, PM and CO 7 sts in alternating colors. PM and begin knitting again across the second sleeve. The two sleeves are now joined with steeks and are worked in the round to the end.

Continue working in Lattice pattern as established, shaping the caps, according to size, as follows. For these directions, references to *left* and *right* are as-oriented; *right* is the beginning of a row, and *left* is the end of a row.

Double Decrease Round: K3tog over the first three sts at *right* edge; SSSK over last three sts at *left* edge. 2 sts removed at each edge.

Decrease Round: K2tog over the first two sts at *right* edge; SSK over last two sts at *left* edge. 1 st removed at each edge.

32: Work a Double Decrease Round every row four times; work a Decrease Round every row five times, then every second and third round three times, then every other round four times, then every round four times; work a Double Decrease Row every row four times. 26 sts.

36: Work a Double Decrease Round every round five times; work a Decrease Round every round eight times, then every second and third round five times, then every round four times; work a Double Decrease Row every round four times. 28 sts.

46 | Fia Pullover

Sleeve

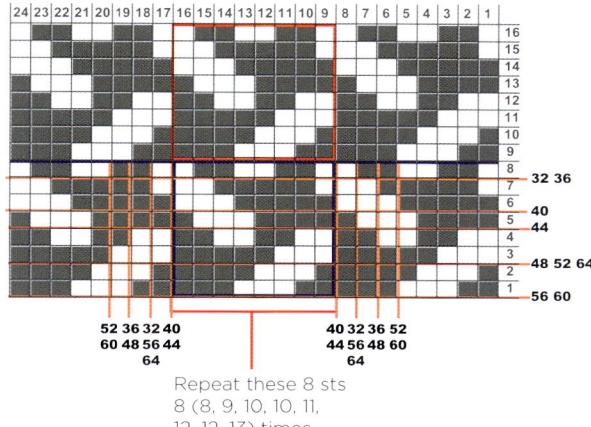

Repeat these 8 sts
8 (8, 9, 10, 10, 11, 12, 12, 13) times.

All charts are followed from bottom to top. When knitting in the round read all rows from right to left as RS rows. When knitting flat, RS rows are read from right to left, and WS rows from left to right.

Begin on first round and stitch indicated for your size. Work repeats as shown.

Work these repeats as shown over entire Sleeve and Sleeve Cap, working Sleeve and Cap shaping as given in the written directions.

40: Work a Double Decrease Round every round five times; work a Decrease Round every round six times, then every second and third round six times, then every round four times; work a Double Decrease Row every row five times. 28 sts.

44: Work a Double Decrease Round every round six times; work a Decrease Round every round eight times, then every other round 11 times, then every round seven times; work a Double Decrease Row every row four times. 36 sts.

48: Work a Double Decrease Round every round seven times; work a Decrease Round every round nine times, then every second and third round three times, then every other round 5 times, then every round ten times; work a Double Decrease Row every row four times. 38 sts.

52: Work a Double Decrease Round every round eight times; work a Decrease Round every round ten times, then every second and third round four times, then every other round three times, then every round eight times; work a Double Decrease Row every row eight times. 42 sts.

56: Work a Double Decrease Round every round ten times; work a Decrease Round every round 12 times, then every second and third round four times, then every other round five times, then every round six times; work a Double Decrease Row every row eight times. 40 sts.

60: Work a Double Decrease Round every round ten times; work a Decrease Round every round 11 times, then every second and third round three times, then every other round seven times, then every round seven times; work a Double Decrease Row every row ten times. 46 sts.

64: Work a Double Decrease Round every round 11 times; work a Decrease Round every round 15 times, then every second and third round three times, then every other round eight times, then every round five times; work a Double Decrease Row every row ten times. 48 sts.

After the last round of the Sleeve Cap, BO all sts in MC.

Body

Like the Sleeves, the body of the pullover begins with a Garter stitch border and is worked in one piece in the round. Steeks are cast on at the armscyes and front neck so that the body can be knit in the round to the shoulders.

All shaping in the Body occurs on either side of columns of stitches at the underarms, just as done in the sleeves. Work all shaping at the same time as working from the Body and Neckline charts; all sizes work through round 145 of the Body chart, then work directions for your size from the Neckline chart. Stitches are bound off on the first round of the Neckline chart – see Neckline section for more instructions.

With smaller needles and MC, CO 272 (312, 344, 368, 392, 436, 472, 504, 528) sts. PM and join to work in the round, being careful not to twist sts. The beginning of the round is the left underarm. Work Garter st around, placing marker after 136 (156, 172, 184, 196, 218, 236, 252, 264) sts to mark right underarm. Work for 1.5" in Garter st.

Switch to larger needles. Attach CC and begin Body patterning: *K1 in MC, work from Body Pattern chart to st before next marker, K1 in MC; rep from * across back. The first and last MC sts on each side are not included on the charts.

Continue working around body in pattern as established, and at the same time, work waist decreases and increases as follows:

Waist Decrease Round: *SSK in MC, work in pattern to 2 sts before next M, K2tog in MC, SM; rep from * to end of round. 4 sts decreased.

Waist Increase Round: *K1 in MC, M1L in pattern, work in pattern to 2 st before next M, M1R in pattern, K1 in MC, SM; rep from * to end of round. 4 sts increased.

Work a Waist Decrease Round every 9th (6th, 5th, 7th, 8th, 10th, 12th, 12th, 18th) round 6 (10, 12, 11, 10, 7, 7, 7, 5) times: 248 (272, 296, 324, 352, 408, 444, 476, 508) sts.

Work 15 (13, 16, 8, 8, 20, 10, 14, 10) rounds in pattern.

Work a Waist Increase Round on the next round, then every 10th (7th, 7th, 8th, 10th, 9th, 10th, 14th, 22nd) round 5 (7, 8, 7, 5, 6, 5, 3, 2) times: 272 (304, 332, 356 372, 436, 468, 492, 520) sts around the body.

Body (continued)

36 Begin armscye

32 Begin armscye

48 | Fia Pullover

Body

Begin on round 1 at the stitch indicated for your size. Work repeats and center motif as shown.

Continue through round 145 of this chart, then move to Neckline chart, working waist and armscye shaping as given in the written directions.

Repeat these 8 sts 4 (6, 7, 7, 9, 10, 11, 12, 12) times.

Repeat these 8 sts 4 (6, 7, 7, 9, 10, 11, 12, 12) times.

Fia Pullover | 49

Neckline (continued)

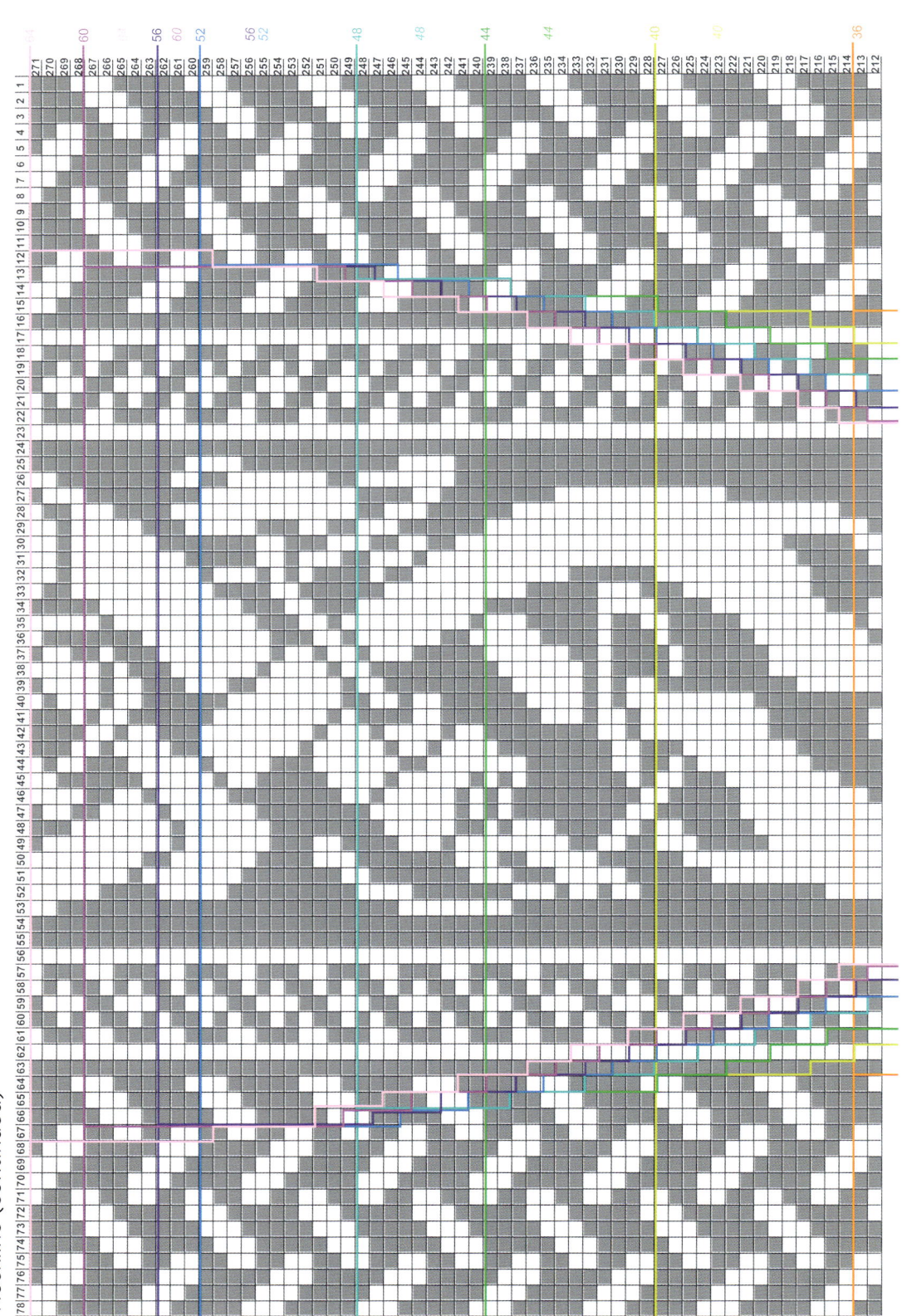

50 | Fia Pullover

Neckline

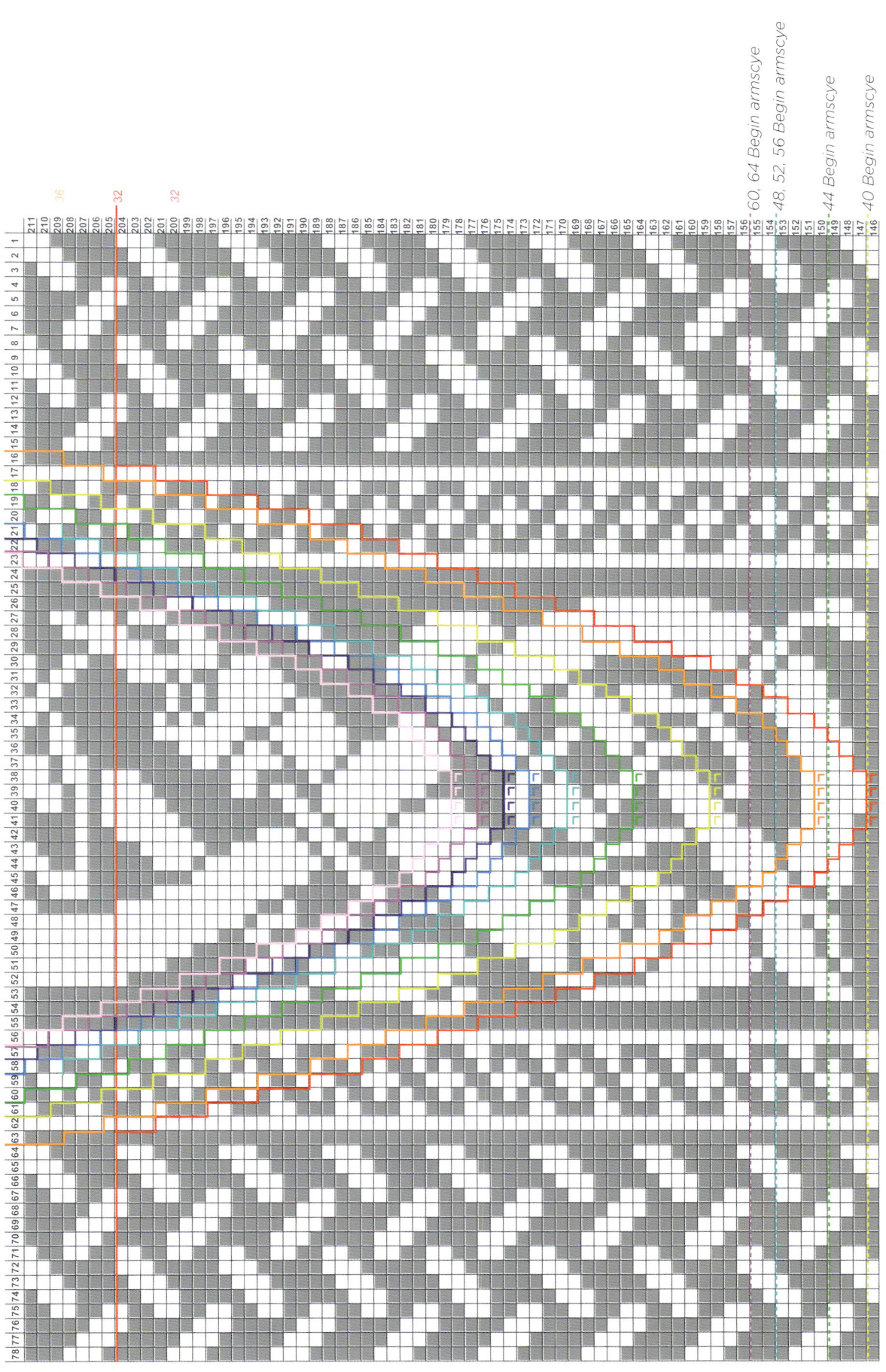

On the round indicated for your size with ⌐ ⌐ BO 4 sts at the front neck. On the next round, cast on a new 7-st steek at the neckline edge.

Decreases at the neckline are shown with the colored line that corresponds to your size. When the line moves over one stitch, work a decrease: SSK over the last two sts at the left neckline edge, and K2tog over the first two sts at the right neckline edge. (Left and right are as worn.)

Work neckline shaping on the front only; work across all Back sts in pattern.

A line runs across the chart indicating the last pattern row for your size; the corresponding size number in italics lines up with the beginning of the shoulder shaping instructions (in written directions).

60, 64 Begin armscye
48, 52, 56 Begin armscye
44 Begin armscye
40 Begin armscye

Fia Pullover | 51

Work 10 (12, 12, 6, 13, 7, 7, 13, 9) rounds in pattern. On the next round, begin shaping armscyes.

Armscyes

Neckline shaping begins during the Armscye shaping. Read through both sections before continuing.

Work across the next round of the Body to 6 (6, 7, 8, 8, 14, 16, 16, 16, 22) sts before Right Underarm Marker; BO the next 12 (12, 14, 16, 16, 28, 32, 32, 32, 44) sts, removing marker. Continue in pattern to the last 6 (6, 7, 8, 8, 14, 16, 16, 16, 22) sts of the round. BO the last 5 (5, 6, 7, 7, 13, 15, 15, 15, 21) charted sts and the last MC st of the round, then BO the first MC st of the next round and 5 (5, 6, 7, 7, 13, 15, 15, 15, 21) charted sts of the second round of the Armscye. Continue across the Front to the last live st.

Cast on a steek at the armscye: CO 7 sts in alternating colors. Join to the next live st of the back and continue across the back to the next bound off st; again, CO 7 sts in alternating colors. Join to the next live st of the front, and continue following decreases in the directions below. Continue to work these steek stitches in a 1x1 checkerboard pattern to the shoulders.

Continue working Body as established, shaping the armscyes as follows. For these directions, references to *left* and *right* are as-oriented; *right* is the beginning of a side (Front or Back), and *left* is the end of a side (Front or Back).

Double Decrease Round: *K3tog over the first three sts at *right* edge; SSSK over last three sts at *left* edge, SM. Repeat from * to end. 2 sts removed at each edge of each side; 8 sts total removed.

Decrease Round: *K2tog over the first two sts at *right* edge; SSK over last two sts at *left* edge, SM. Repeat from * to end. 1 st removed at each edge of each side; 4 sts total removed.

32: Work a Double Decrease Round on the first round; work a Decrease Round every round twice, then every other round twice, then every third round twice, then every fifth round twice. 40 armscye sts removed, 10 at each edge.

36: Work a Double Decrease Round on the first round; work a Decrease Round every round five times, then every other round twice, then every third round twice, then every fifth round twice. 52 armscye sts removed, 13 at each edge.

40: Work a Double Decrease Round every round twice; work a Decrease Round every round three times, then every other round three times, then every third round twice, then every fifth round twice. 56 armscye sts removed, 14 at each edge.

44: Work a Double Decrease Round every round four times; work a Decrease Round every round five times, then every other round five times, then every third round twice, then on the fifth round. 76 armscye sts removed, 19 at each edge.

48: Work a Double Decrease Round every round five times; work a Decrease Round every round seven times, then every other round five times, then every third round twice, then on the fifth round. 100 armscye sts removed, 25 at each edge.

52: Work a Double Decrease Round every round four times; work a Decrease Round every round seven times, then every other round four times, then every fourth round twice, then on the fifth round. 104 armscye sts removed, 26 at each edge.

56: Work a Double Decrease Round every round six times; work a Decrease Round every round seven times, then every other round six times, then every fourth round twice. 108 armscye sts removed, 27 at each edge.

60: Work a Double Decrease Round every round eight times; work a Decrease Round every round twelve times, then every other round twice, then on the fifth round. 124 armscye sts removed, 31 at each edge.

64: Work a Double Decrease Round every round eight times; work a Decrease Round every round 11 times, then every other round three times, then every third round three times, then on the sixth round. 136 armscye sts removed, 34 at each edge.

Neckline

Like the Armscyes, after binding off for the neckline, a steek is cast on across the gap. On the round shown for your size of the Neckline chart, BO the center four sts to begin the V-neck opening. When you reach that first bound off st in the next round, cast on a 7-st steek like those for the armscyes and rejoin to the right side of the Front. Work Neckline decreases as shown in the chart at the same time as shaping the Armscyes.

After the Armscye and Neckline shaping are complete, 116, 126, 138, 140, 146, 166, 180, 184, 192) sts remain across each front and back, not counting steek sts.

Shoulder shaping

A few rounds before the end of the chart for your size, begin shaping the shoulders on the Front and Back. You will work across the Front only first, then attach yarn to work across the Back in the same manner.

Work to round 200 (209, 223, 235, 244, 255, 256, 261, 265). On this round, knit to 12 (12, 13, 15, 15, 16, 11, 11, 11) sts before the end of the right Front; Wrap and Turn (see *Notes*). Purl back in pattern to 12 (12, 13, 15, 15, 16, 11, 11, 11) sts before the end of the left Front, W&T. *Knit in pattern to 12 (12, 13, 15, 15, 16, 11, 11, 11) sts before the wrapped st on the right Front shoulder, W&T. Purl to 12 (12, 13, 15, 15, 16, 11, 11, 11) sts before the wrapped st on the left Front shoulder, W&T. * Sizes 56 (60, 64): repeat between *s once more.

All sizes: Knit to the last st of the left Front shoulder. Break CC, and knit to the end of the right shoulder, picking up wraps and knitting them together with the sts they wrap (see *Notes*). Purl back across right shoulder, BO the neckline steek sts, and purl across left shoulder, picking up wraps and purling them together with the sts they wrap. Place live sts on a holder or scrap yarn.

Holding the Back with RS facing, attach yarn and begin working from Shoulder Shaping directions as done for the front; on the last row of MC, BO the center 46 (48, 48, 50, 52, 54, 54, 54, 56) back neck sts.

Finishing

Turn the sweater inside out. Place matching front and back shoulders on needles, holding one side in front of the other, right sides together. With CC, perform a 3-needle BO across all sts. Repeat for other shoulder.

To finish the sweater, the steeks must first be sewn and cut. Then, the sleeves are sewn in, and the collar is picked up and knit on.

Preparing Hand-Sewn Steeks

The cut line will be directly in the center of the steek; a line of stitching one st to each side of this cut line will help to stabilize the cut edge. It may help to use a contrasting color of thread; this will not be visible in the finished piece.

Hold work so that the steek is in the center of the piece. Reach in and smooth any yarn ends away from this stitch. Lay piece on a flat surface to help with sewing.

With sewing needle and thread, sew a running stitch between the first and second sts to the right of the center cut line. Be sure to catch the floats between every stitch; sew right through the yarn. Turn work and backstitch down the same column of stitches. To backstitch, run the needle under and out as a normal stitch, but begin the next stitch halfway between the beginning and end of the first. This will create little loops of thread in the fabric that can't be pulled out. Be sure to make many tiny stitches and pierce the yarn with each stitch if possible. Do not pull the thread so tight as to pucker the fabric. The more time you take in this step, the stronger the edge will be!

Repeat the sewn line one stitch to the left of the center cut line. Cut through center column of sts carefully with very sharp scissors.

Repeat these directions on sleeve steeks, center front and neckline steeks, and armscye steeks.

Set in Sleeves

With right sides facing out, set sleeves into armscye openings, making sure that the center of each sleeve cap is placed at the shoulder seam and that the bound off stitches for both sleeve and armscye are centered. Pin in place. Using yarn needle and yarn, begin at the underarm and sew sleeves into the armscyes, using mattress stitch.

Collar

The collar is picked up and knit around the neckline; it is worked in Garter st.

Hold sweater with RS facing. With smaller needles and MC, PU and knit around the neckline, starting at the right edge of the Back neck: 46 (48, 48, 50, 52, 54, 54, 54, 56) back neck sts to shoulder join, PM, PU and knit 44 (48, 52, 56, 60, 66, 66, 68, 70) sts to center front, PM, PU and K and 44 (48, 52, 56, 60, 66, 66, 68, 70) sts up to the Back neck. 134 (144, 152, 162, 172, 186, 186, 190, 196) sts. PM and join to work in the round.

Purl one round.

Begin Collar Shaping:
Round 1: SSK, (K to 2 sts before M, K2tog) twice, SSK, K to end.
Round 2: Purl to first M, SM, P2tog, (P to 2 sts before M, SSP) twice.

Repeat these two rounds 8 times.

Loosely BO all sts.

Weave in ends. Wash and block.

18.5 (18.5, 18.5, 18.75, 19, 19, 19.25, 19.25, 19)"

23 (24, 25.5, 26.75, 27.75, 29, 29, 29.5, 30)"

34 (38, 41.5, 45.5, 49.5, 54.5, 58, 62, 65.5)"

Abbreviations

BO	bind off		and back of stitch	PU	pick up	SSP	sl, sl, p these 2 sts tog tbl
cn	cable needle	K-wise	knitwise	P-wise	purlwise	SSSK	sl, sl, sl, k these 3 sts tog
CC	contrast color	LH	left hand	rep	repeat		
CDD	Centered double dec	M	marker	Rev St st	reverse stockinette stitch	St st	stockinette stitch
CO	cast on	M1	make one stitch	RH	right hand	sts	stitch(es)
cont	continue	M1L	make one left-leaning stitch	rnd(s)	round(s)	TBL	through back loop
dec	decrease(es)	M1R	make one right-leaning stitch	RS	right side	TFL	through front loop
DPN(s)	double pointed needle(s)	MC	main color	Sk	skip	tog	together
		P	purl	Sk2p	sl 1, k2tog, pass slipped stitch over k2tog: 2 sts dec	W&T	wrap & turn (see specific instructions in pattern)
EOR	every other row	P2tog	purl 2 sts together				
inc	increase	PM	place marker	SKP	sl, k, psso: 1 st dec	WE	work even
K	knit	PFB	purl into the front and back of stitch	SL	slip	WS	wrong side
K2tog	knit two sts together			SM	slip marker	WYIB	with yarn in back
KFB	knit into the front	PSSO	pass slipped stitch over	SSK	sl, sl, k these 2 sts tog	WYIF	with yarn in front
						YO	yarn over

54

Knit Picks®

Knit Picks yarn is both luxe and affordable—a seeming contradiction trounced! But it's not just about the pretty colors; we also care deeply about fiber quality and fair labor practices, leaving you with a gorgeously reliable product you'll turn to time and time again.

THIS COLLECTION FEATURES

Palette
Fingering Weight
100% Peruvian Highland Wool

Wool of the Andes Worsted
Worsted Weight
100% Peruvian Highland Wool

Chroma Worsted
Worsted Weight
70% Wool, 30% Nylon

Gloss DK
DK Weight
70% Merino Wool, 30% Silk

Wool of the Andes Tweed
Worsted Weight
80% Peruvian Highland Wool, 20% Donegal Tweed

View these beautiful yarns and more at www.KnitPicks.com